The Jerusalem Jesus Knew

An Archaeological Guide to the Gospels

John Wilkinson

The Jerusalem Jesus Knew
An Archaeological Guide to the Gospels

with 101 photographs and 42 diagrams

Thomas Nelson Publishers
Nashville • Camden • New York

For John Cottrell
in gratitude and admiration

Published in the United States in Nashville, Tennessee, by Thomas Nelson,
Inc., and distributed in Canada by Lawson Falle, Ltd., Cambridge,
Ontario. First American printing in paperback: 1983.

Library of Congress Cataloging in Publication Data

Wilkinson, John, 1929-
  The Jerusalem Jesus knew.

  Previously published as: Jerusalem as Jesus knew it.
1978.
  Bibliography: p.
  Includes index.
  1. Jerusalem—Antiquities.   2. Jesus Christ—Biography
—Passion Week.   3. Bible. N.T.—Antiquities.
4. Christian biography—Palestine.   I. Title.
DS109.W7 1983   933   83-8096
ISBN 0-8407-5856-1 (pbk.)

Printed in the United States of America

1 2 3 4 5 6 7 8 9 10—85 84 83

Contents

Acknowledgments for Photographs

Photographs are the property of the author with the following exceptions

Elia Photo-Service 22
Garo Jerusalem 128
Stuart Inglis and John Wilkinson 38, 43, 46, 56, 62, 64, 74, 82, 89, 90, 93, 96, 98, 105, 112, 114, 121, 122, 142, 143
John Landgraf 108
Museum of the Flagellation, Jerusalem 31, 32, 33, 34, 35, 36, 67
Rockefeller Museum 69
Supreme Muslim Council 55, 58, 65
Yergatian Jerusalem 24

Preface

Nine years in Jerusalem have changed my attitudes to the city a good deal. Particularly I am surprised by the number of physical remains in the city which have survived from the time of Jesus. By describing them I hope to sketch in something of the background against which Jesus worked.

I am specially grateful to two people: to Dr Robert J. Fortna, through whose encouragement I embarked on this book, and to Father Pierre Benoit O.P. To his work I feel I probably owe most of the good points (and none of the mistakes) made in the following pages.

I also wish to thank Dr Stuart Inglis for taking the air photographs, Mr Albert Storme of the Museum of the Flagellation for the very kind way in which he helped me obtain photographs of coins, and Elia Photo-Service for their meticulous processing. My thanks to the Armenian Superior in the Church of the Holy Sepulchre and to the Director of the Museum of the Flagellation for permission to take photographs. To Mrs Helen Assad, who very kindly added the typing of the manuscript to her other work in the height of summer, I am very grateful indeed. It would have been impossible for me to write the book at all without the generous help given in every way by my wife Alix.

I am also most grateful to Mr F. Johnson, Mr R. Scanlon, and Dr Yoram Tsafrir, and to others who have helped me to put right some of my errors and oversights in the first impression.

Introduction

The aim of the present book is to explore Jesus' relationship with the Jerusalem of his day. But can such an aim be achieved? Are we confident that we can even discover definite information about Jesus of Nazareth, let alone about the city as it was in about A D 30?

Some of that Jerusalem is now invisible because it lies buried deep beneath the buildings and streets of the present day, and much of it is irrevocably destroyed. But when we turn to the life of Jesus, what can we expect to find? Archaeology is not likely to help very much, since he built no monuments. We learn a great deal more, both from what was written down and eventually accepted by the Christian community round the world as the New Testament, and what was remembered by the community in Jerusalem whose members showed visitors the places where they believed Jesus had been. But still very large gaps are left. Thus we seem to know no single fact about Jesus' life between the time when he was twelve and the period when he was 'about thirty' (see Luke II:42, III:23).

The core of the written record, so far as we are concerned in this book, is to be found in the four Gospels. We therefore need to bear in mind when we use them that there was no such form of writing as a 'Gospel' till the first of the four was written. A Gospel is not exactly a 'Life of Jesus', for a 'Life' or biography would have to tell us all sorts of personal details about him. Indeed we find that some of the Christians of early days were thoroughly dissatisfied with the Gospels as we have them, because they failed to answer so many questions of biographical interest. What was Jesus like as a boy? What did he learn at school? And what did he look like as a grown man? Of the four Gospel writers Luke comes nearest to showing an interest in subjects of this kind, but often even he tells us very little (see Luke II:40).

As if in protest there grew up, perhaps at almost the same time as the Gospels, a collection of pamphlets and tracts which claimed to supply all the answers. 'Apocryphal Gospels', as they are usually called, provided not only an abundance of the personal details which had somehow failed to find their way into the officially approved Gospels, but also put into Jesus' mouth teachings which were in line with the beliefs of unorthodox groups like the Gnostics. Despite its popular appeal this literature seems mostly to have been pure fiction, and was frequently condemned as such.

The Gospels are not biographies. Nor indeed are they objective, complete records of the kind we expect from careful modern writers who report events with a scholarly attention to detail. The writers' attitude to Jesus is one of commitment, and their intention is missionary. The Gospels are therefore intended as propaganda in the best sense of that word: thus John tells us that he was writing 'that you may believe that Jesus is the Messiah, the Son of God, and that believing you may have life in his name' (Ch. XX:31). The primary concern of the Gospel writers was with a spiritual belief, not just a material truth, even though the material existence of Jesus was the means by which the spiritual truth was given its expression.

Who were these Gospel writers? Today's equivalent of saying 'Matthew, Mark, Luke and John' would be 'John Smith, Peter Jones, David Robinson, and Michael Brown', names which appear by the dozen in every telephone directory. Plenty of Matthews, Marks, Lukes, and Johns were about in the first century A D, and merely to have names like these does not tell us who they were.

Needless to say, the early Christians identified the Gospel writers with the people of the same names who are mentioned in the New Testament. If their identifications are correct, then the writers may have been eyewitnesses of many of the things they describe: so Mark is identified with the John Mark who lived in Jerusalem (see Acts XII:12), Matthew and John with the apostles (Mark III:18, I:19), and Luke, rightly, with Paul's friend (Colossians IV:14). But the New Testament itself does not make these identifications, and one of our earliest witnesses outside the New Testament speaks in a way which makes this unlikely in the case of Mark. This is a writer called Papias, who probably died in about A D 130, who tells us that Mark (and he does not say John Mark) became Peter's 'translator' or 'interpreter', and 'wrote down accurately all the memories he told him'. The impression left is that Mark the Gospel writer was entirely dependent on Peter for his information,

9

and so was probably not a member of the same group as the apostles themselves.

Matthew and Luke appear to have taken material both from Mark and from a second source other than Mark's Gospel, since there are passages in these two Gospels, not based on Mark, where they agree closely (compare for instance Luke III:17–18 with Matthew III:12, or Luke VII:18–23 with Matthew XI:2–6). This source is usually identified by the letter Q, short for *Quelle,* the German for 'fountain' or 'source'. Each of these writers also reproduces material which does not appear in the other (see for instance Matthew XVI:17–20, or Luke XV:11–32).

Anyone who has to read histories written in antiquity is well accustomed to occasions when they are not in agreement; and, as we might expect, the four Gospels are no exception. They are consistent in their missionary intention, to pass on their deep reverence for the Messiah Jesus and his work, but each Gospel writer has his unique approach, and his own way of arranging and presenting his material. Furthermore, there are various points of disagreement, and in this book we will grapple with some of these passages at the level of historical detail. Some people are seriously disturbed by the very possibility of such disagreements in Holy Scripture. But to the present writer those in the Gospels seem slight in comparison to many found in non-Christian writings of the same period that they should have no bearing on the acceptability of the Christian faith.

We ought not to call the second Gospel 'The Life of Jesus by Mark'. But perhaps we might call it 'Jesus and his Campaign—a personal testimony by Mark'. We may expect in this and in the other three Gospels to find a generally reliable picture of parts of Jesus' life and work, even if we encounter occasional difficulties over questions of detail. Let us now move away from the Gospels and examine what we can grasp of the unwritten memories of the Christian community in Jerusalem.

The average visitor to Jerusalem today is shown so many 'holy places' connected with Jesus that he cannot help at some stage asking himself whether they are all genuine. It can be disturbing to find (for instance) two places pointed out, both of which are said to have been Jesus' tomb. So people sometimes wash their hands of the holy places and take comfort in generalities, like 'Jesus certainly knew this landscape', or 'Jesus certainly walked on these hills'. Obviously it is easier to remember people we have known when we visit the places where they belonged. At the very least the places where Jesus Christ lived and did his work ought to help us to picture him. Moreover, we know that Jesus of Nazareth moved about and did his work in the general area of Galilee and Jerusalem. To visit and to study this area is to learn about the environment he knew; and as we too come to know it we may learn how it affected him and the form in which he expressed his message.

In Jerusalem many Christian holy places are shown to visitors. Are any of them the same as the ones mentioned in the Bible? Certainly. For if the Gospel writers worked in the way we have suggested they would have been able to ask local people where certain things were done by Jesus. Would the writers have had any interest in asking such questions, and would the local people have wanted to remember the different places? Probably, yes. The interest of the writers may be gauged by the fact that they mention a good number of places by name in the course of describing Christ's ministry. Such and such an event took place in the synagogue at Capernaum, or at Bethesda, or in Solomon's Porch. And we know that from early times local people pointed out the holy places to visitors. Thus before A D 130 (when he left the Holy Land for good) Justin Martyr was informed of a cave in Bethlehem where Jesus was said to have been born. Or, again, the apocryphal Acts of John, written soon after A D 200, when it mentions a cave on the Mount of Olives, speaks of it in a way that suggests the cave was already revered as the place of Christ's teaching (see Matthew XXIV:3) and of his Ascension (Acts I:6–12).

These hints do not lead us very far. Thus we are not equipped to make a complete list of the earliest holy places that were visited in Jerusalem, nor to describe in any detail the way in which they were viewed by the Christian community. At least they show that the Christians of the Holy Land had begun to point out the holy places from an early date; and though our first full-scale account of pilgrimage in Jerusalem was not written till 333, it probably mentions some places which had been pointed out from early times. Of these some might be authentic, even though others are obviously fictitious or wrongly located. But although the earliest local traditions may include some correct information, we are less likely to gain authentic information about biblical Jerusalem from traditions of later origin. As a rule of thumb we should regard a holy place first pointed out after A D 400 as more likely to be an imaginary addition to the topography of Jerusalem than a correct identification.

We discover a great deal about Jesus from the Gospels, and may find out some facts about the Jerusalem of his time through local traditions.

But when both types of study have been done there are plenty of gaps and blanks. How far can we hope that archaeology will help us to fill them?

Local weather conditions dictate part of our answer, for in all the places mentioned in the Gospels there is a rainy winter, with the single exception of the Jericho and Dead Sea area. Except in this district there are no organic remains from the time of Jesus, for they have rotted away. Thus from Jerusalem we have no cloth, so it is hard to know what clothes people wore, and no parchment or papyrus, so we are severely restricted in our knowledge of their affairs and literature. Here and there organic materials have been protected against humidity in some airtight container or space, such as a jar or a tomb chamber. But in only one place can we expect complete preservation. This region lies along the coast of the Dead Sea, which accounts for the important finds made there like the Dead Sea scrolls and the finds connected with Masada and Bar Cochba's cave at Nahal Hever.

Even though in Jerusalem the wood of roofs and furniture has disappeared there are many places throughout the country where we can see the walls, and therefore know the size and plan, of ancient buildings. By studying them we can learn something of the pattern of family life and life in the community, which is valuable background material for the study of the Gospels. But only in a very few cases can we say to whom a building belonged: such identifiable buildings are usually either large monuments mentioned in literature, which can be identified by their position (such as the retaining wall of the Temple area in Jerusalem), or buildings which happened to be identified by inscriptions cut into stone or set in mosaic (for example the inscription identifying the synagogue of Theodotus). It is undoubtedly one of archaeology's great gifts to the historian that it can reveal buildings, and usually also say when they were built and occupied. But having given so much it can often give no more.

Jesus, as an itinerant preacher and healer, is hardly likely to have set up inscriptions or erected monuments. Thus archaeology is unlikely to provide much which has a direct relationship to him as an individual. But it can shed a good deal of light on the world in which he lived.

The Background

Life in the Provinces

Ideally we should expect to understand more about Jesus' work if we could acquire precise knowledge of the historical events which took place during his lifetime, but we do not know the exact dates for the beginning and ending of his life on earth. Even if we did, they would not be of very great significance, because we know the events of local history at this time only sketchily, and most of our knowledge seems to have little direct bearing on his ministry.

Matthew II:16 described Herod the Great as killing the children in the region of Bethlehem soon after Jesus was born. Thus Matthew implies that Jesus' birth was before Herod's death, which occurred in March or April, 4 BC. Luke II:1-2, on the other hand, links the birth with the census of Quirinius, which was held at an important turning point in local history and occurred in AD 6. These two dates, being ten years apart, cannot both be correct, though either might be. We know that Jesus' trial was conducted by Caiaphas and Pilate, so it cannot have been held before AD 26 when Pilate became prefect of Judaea nor after AD 36 when Caiaphas died and Pilate was recalled to Rome. If Luke is right therefore in another passage, where he tells us that Jesus when he began his public ministry was 'about thirty years of age' (Luke III:23), we seem to have another ten-year span of uncertainty. Two clues, however, suggest that we should look for a date early in the time available: one, unexpectedly provided by Luke himself, Ch. III:1, that Jesus' public ministry began 'in the fifteenth year of the reign of Tiberius Caesar', which could mean either AD 26 or 28; and the other, provided by John II:20, where it appears, again at the opening of Jesus' public ministry, that the Temple had been under construction for forty-six years, again indicating AD 26.

Let us assume, for the purposes of visualizing the background of Jesus' life, that he was born early in 4 BC, began his public ministry at the age of twenty-nine in AD 26, and after working in Galilee for three years came to Jerusalem for the final events of his life in AD 29 or 30. He would thus have been born half-way through the immensely long reign of Augustus Caesar, and just before the death of Herod the Great. Quarrels between Herod's sons soon brought about a split in the Jewish kingdom, which the Romans eventually divided among three princes; Philip (who does not concern us); Archelaus, who, as the senior of the three, was entitled ethnarch; and Antipas, who came to be called Herod probably in AD 6. Herod Antipas remained as ruler of Galilee during the rest of Jesus' lifetime, and Luke's Gospel says that he took part in Jesus' trial. But Archelaus, who ruled Judaea and Samaria, was made the subject of complaint to Augustus by a joint Jewish-Samaritan delegation, and banished for disobedience to the Emperor. His departure in AD 6 meant that the heartland of the Jewish kingdom was reduced to a minor province of the Roman empire, and on this occasion it became administratively necessary for Quirinius to conduct his census, and assess the new provincial population for tax. When Quirinius, who was the senior official responsible for the large and important province of Syria, went away, the oversight of Judaea and Samaria (often loosely called Judaea) was entrusted to a governor with the title of procurator.

Practically nothing is known either of the first procurator or of his successors until we come to Pilate. Under the first of them, Coponius, there was a revolt against Rome by Judas of Galilee (see Acts V:37). Coponius and his two successors served for three-year periods. But in AD 14 Augustus died and was succeeded by Tiberius, who changed the appointment, altering the governor's rank from procurator to prefect and extending the length of service. Valerius Gratus, who was appointed prefect in AD 15, served for eleven years. He made a memorable beginning by deposing four high priests in Jerusalem, of whom he himself had appointed three. Caiaphas, the high priest he appointed in AD 18, was evidently a more suitable choice, since he remained in office for eighteen years. If Jesus lived at the time we have suggested, therefore, he was probably conscious of Judas' revolt and its suppression, since he would then have been nine years old. At least he must have experienced it as a time of disturbance. He could have drawn more mature conclusions both about Roman rule and about the nature of the high priesthood during the governorship of Gratus, for by AD 18 he would have been twenty-one years of age.

1 View from the south end of Mt Meron, the summit of Upper Galilee. Although the Mediterranean and Mt Carmel, in the distance, are only 45 kilometres (28 miles) away, Galilee was cut off from the sea by the province of Phoenicia

Jesus in his early years visited Jerusalem only occasionally. As a boy he was brought up mostly in the provincial environment of the small and insignificant village of Nazareth. Thus if we are to be aware of the meaning of his work in Jerusalem we need, for two reasons, to take a rapid glance at Galilee: first because it formed the basis of his own experience, and second because the particular qualities of Jerusalem are more easily pictured if we find some material of the same period for comparison and contrast.

Galilee was provincial in two ways. On the one hand it was a client principality and its people had no direct relationship with Rome except through Antipas, its tetrarch. It was also geographically remote from Rome. Indeed the journey would take perhaps two months by sea, and could take fifteen by land. But on the other hand Galilee was remote from the capital cities of its own area. Caesarea, which was the seat of the prefect, the senior Roman representative in the neighbourhood, was more than a day's journey from any place in Galilee, and although a prefect assigned to Judaea had no official responsibilities in Galilee we can hardly believe that he was without influence there. Galilee, moreover, was about three days away from the Jewish religious and cultural capital, Jerusalem.

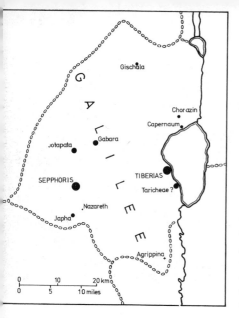

2 *Centres of population in ancient Galilee. The black circles indicate the relative sizes, Sepphoris containing about 50,000 and Gischala about 9,000 inhabitants. Nazareth, as a small village, may have had only about 500*

Galilee, though surrounded by cities of some repute at the time of Jesus' birth, contained only one city which could be regarded as their equal: this was Sepphoris, about five miles from Nazareth. In the troubles which followed the death of Herod the Great in 4 BC, Josephus tells us, the Roman general Varus 'burnt the city and reduced its inhabitants to slavery'. But Antipas soon re-fortified it 'to be the ornament of all Galilee and called it "The Imperial" (Autocratoris)'. This renewed and probably impressive phase of the city was the one Jesus would have known. Later on, however, after Tiberius' accession, Antipas followed the example of his father, Herod the Great, and founded a new capital city, to which he gave the name Tiberias and privileges even greater than those of Sepphoris. Yet for Josephus the glory of Galilee was not its urban developments, but its agriculture. 'It is everywhere so rich in soil and pasturage,' he says, 'and produces such a variety of trees, that work seems easy enough to attract even the lazy. In fact the inhabitants have cultivated every bit of it, and not a scrap lies idle. So the towns have large numbers of inhabitants, and there are big populations in all the villages on account of this fertility: the smallest of them contains above fifteen thousand inhabitants' (*The Jewish War* 3:42–44).

Of all the territories which made up 'Judaea' – meaning the whole extent of the territories which had been ruled by Herod the Great –

3 Alluvial soil in the fertile Biqa'a Beit Netofa (Sahl el Battuf), 10 kilometres (about 6 miles) west of the Sea of Galilee

Galilee was indeed the most fertile. Its soils, on which Josephus rightly comments, are mainly the terra rossa and Mediterranean brown that are characteristic of many other parts of Palestine. But it has also, near the Sea of Galilee, an area of black basaltic soil, which is the result of volcanic action. Prehistoric eruptions affected an area about 50 kilometres (or 32 miles) from north to south, stretching to Lake Huleh in the north, and south as far as Agrippina: as the basalt eventually decomposed it usually formed excellent soil, but the soil has been washed away from very large tracts of land to the north of the Sea of Galilee, which are today covered with large basalt boulders. Josephus therefore exaggerates when he tells us that 'Galilee is entirely under cultivation' and 'not a scrap lies idle'. These statements may indeed come true when the bulldozer has done its work more thoroughly, but until the invention of large-scale earthmoving equipment there had never been much cultivation on this volcanic dike bordering the north shore of the Sea. We need therefore to give Josephus credit for mentioning pasturage as well as cultivation, and to envisage Jesus in Capernaum as meeting a great many of the shepherds and other herdsmen who worked in the region immediately to the north of his chosen headquarters.

4 *Basalt rocks, which cover the surface of this field just north of biblical Chorazin, have always prevented cultivation*

In the Holy Land good soil is a relatively common asset. The special advantage of Galilee over other districts lay rather in its good rainfall. Ill. 5 shows the contours of the landscape, with the lowest level (marked with dots) around and including the Sea of Galilee. All this area is below Mediterranean sea level, and the surface of the Sea of Galilee itself is 200 metres (650 feet) lower. Because, unlike the Mediterranean or the Red Sea, the Sea of Galilee and the Dead Sea came to form part of a closed system, and their levels, which had once been the same as that of the neighbouring seas, were reduced by evaporation. In fact the surface of the Dead Sea is now 396 metres (nearly 1,300 feet) below the Mediterranean. The part of this area below sea level which appears on Ill. 5 is about 8 kilometres (5 miles) wide, and forms part of the Rift Valley, and the same Valley (though in this case with its floor slightly above sea level) continued northwards on either side of the small Lake Huleh to the north of the Sea of Galilee. Lake Huleh is at present drained, but it existed as a lake in Josephus' time (and till about 1957) and was anciently known as Lake Semechonitis. Traces of the Rift Valley exist for a further two hundred miles to the north, and the Valley itself also extends south, past the Dead Sea, to Aqaba/Eilat, and then (as the Gulf of Aqaba) to join the

Red Sea. The whole rift system, of which the Red Sea is a part, stretches southwards through Africa till it reaches almost as far as the River Zambesi, 6,500 kilometres (4,000 miles) away.

From the Rift Valley with its unusual features, the ground mounts to what, on the left of our simplified contour map, looks like a plain broken with hills to the south and a considerable mountain area to the north. In fact the shape is more broken than here appears, since a good deal of the undulation does not show on the map because the contours are so far apart. They are separated by a vertical interval of 300 metres (nearly 1,000 feet) and the highest point in the mountain area (the white spot at the northern end of the largest dark patch) is Mount Meron, with a height of 1,208 metres, (3,963 feet).

It so happens that in Galilee (though not necessarily in areas further south) the map that shows heights also indicates the increase in the amount of rain that falls each year. Every extra 300 metres (about 1,000 feet) adds about 12 centimetres (5 inches) of rain, and even the minimum (about 40 centimetres; 15 inches) is enough to enable the crops to grow without irrigation, while the maximum (over 102 centimetres; 40 inches) is a plentiful supply by any standards, and produces a luxuriant 'Alpine' landscape. Though the variation in rainfall is considerable in Galilee it is nowhere too low to prevent cultivation.

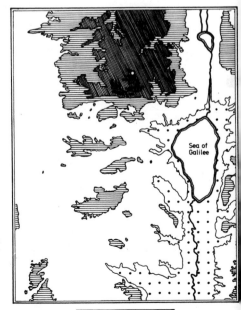

5 Galilee, showing contour lines at 300-metre intervals. The dotted area round the Sea of Galilee is below the level of the Mediterranean

25 kilometres

6 *This chameleon, found at biblical Chorazin in the Rift Valley, is an animal ordinarily found only in subtropical regions*

7 *(right) Papyrus, another subtropical species, can be seen growing in the Rift Valley at Lake Huleh*

8 *(opposite) Olives, fir trees and a palm grow side by side on the Sea of Galilee*

Temperatures, too, cover a wide range. Thus Mount Meron has three months of frost and over six months in the year when the mean temperature is less than 15 °C (59°F). But at Capernaum temperatures as low as this last only for about two months and there is never any frost whereas the summer is both long and hot. For four months the mean temperature is over 25 °C (77°F), and a month of this period is spent with a mean temperature of over 30 °C (86°F) and a maximum of above 35 °C (95°F). These subtropical conditions make possible a wide variety of cultivation including, in modern times, quantities of bananas. Our photographs show natural species of a subtropical type found there; a chameleon, found at biblical Chorazin; and papyrus, which grows on Lake Huleh. But the speciality of the Rift Valley in ancient times was the date palm, which was so important that Herod Antipas pictured it on nearly all his coins. The range of trees which grew beside the Sea of Galilee in the first century AD is indicated by Josephus in these words: 'There is also an area called Gennesaret where there is not a single plant which its fertile soil refuses to produce: those who tend it grow every sort of thing, and the climate has a balance equally welcome to plants of opposite characteristics. So the most winter-loving tree, the walnut, grows there luxuriantly, but so also in that region do date palms, trees which live on heat, and also those which need a more moderate climate, such as figs and olives' (*War* 3 : 516–17). The variety is illustrated by Ills. 8 and 9.

9 A walnut tree grown in the grounds of Kibbutz Dafna, near the north end of the Rift Valley

While it was in some ways exceptional, Galilee also supported farming of the kinds most characteristic of the Holy Land, with its wheat, grapes and olives, producing the 'corn and wine and oil' of so many passages in the Old Testament. But if we conclude from its prosperity that there was a large population, what sort of numbers should we imagine? In 1961 the same area contained about 190,000 persons, probably fewer than in the time of Jesus, because in that year parts of the area were evacuated for military use, and the farms there needed fewer labourers than those of ancient times. Nor at that time were there yet any large industrial concentrations in the area. Josephus informs us that in his day Galilee contained 'three million' inhabitants, which is incredible in view of the fact that the present population of the entire Holy Land is only three and a half million. But, as Josephus' readers soon discover, his more unreasonable figures usually look sensible when divided by ten. Josephus was not good at Greek, and it is quite possible that those who helped him in his Greek composition misunderstood what he had said or written down for them. Thus a simple word like 'three' would be correctly transmitted, but the more unusual numeral 'million' might easily be a mistake for the equally unusual 'hundred thousand'. Let us therefore suppose that Josephus intended to write 300,000, and see if such a statement makes sense.

Here and there Josephus gives us some facts and figures which help us to check the total for Galilee as a whole. Thus he tells us that Sepphoris (as rebuilt and enlarged by Antipas between 3 BC and AD 8–10) was the largest 'city' in Galilee. Probably, then, it was about comparable in population with Jerusalem at this period, and contained about 50,000 persons. Eventually Tiberias, founded in AD 19–20 half-way through Jesus' lifetime, grew to a comparable size, and had doubtless done so by the time Josephus was there. Gabara, though Josephus once classes it with Sepphoris and Tiberias as one of the three chief cities, was certainly smaller than Sepphoris, and we should probably class it with Taricheae and Jotapata which, if we follow Josephus' figures, probably had about 40,000 each. The largest 'village' of Galilee, Japha, had a population which Josephus tells us amounted to 17,130 persons, and he seems to imply that the population of Gischala numbered 9,000. This would seem a reasonable estimate also for Chorazin (Khirbet Kherazeh?) and Capernaum, to judge from their remains. Since Josephus also tells us that Galilee contained 204 villages, and assuming an average population of 500, we can estimate the total population of Galilee in his time. On the basis we have suggested it would be 365,000, which is not too far from the 300,000 that was our guess above.

The main centres of population are marked on Ill. 2 by circles of different sizes, each representing the relative size of the population. Who were these Galileans and how did they live? Here we must remember that the phrase 'Galilee of the Gentiles', which appears in Matthew IV:15, is not a description of Galilee as Jesus knew it. Rather, it is a quotation of Isaiah IX:1, which may perhaps have been accurate as a description of the area eight centuries before. Some Jews

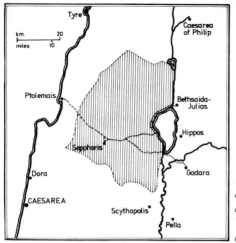

10 The cities in and around Galilee in Jesus' childhood. The new city of Tiberias became important only in about A D *20*

had lived in Galilee during the period of the Maccabees, but they were expelled. Just before 100 BC Galilee was conquered by the Jewish monarch, who not only enabled the Jewish families who had formerly lived there to return, but also presented the non-Jewish population of the district with the alternative of either conversion to Judaism or expulsion. Members of the Jewish religion were evidently powerful in the population of Jesus' time, since their ruler Antipas was unable to depict living beings on his coins, doubtless out of respect for the Jews' feelings for the second of the Ten Commandments, for, in the strict interpretation of those times this command was held to prohibit not only the worship, but also the manufacture of the likeness of any created being.

We know surprisingly little about main roads in Galilee in ancient times, and in all probability the one going from Ptolemais to the Sea of Galilee was the only one of major importance. It approached Sepphoris from the north-west, and after passing slightly to the north went on eastwards, probably for about a further 10 kilometres (6 miles) to the site now occupied by the village of Tur'an. There it forked, the southern branch descending to cross the Jordan, skirt the south end of the Lake, and then climb to Gadara, while the northern branch went straight on to join the Lake at the site of Tiberias and there turned left to skirt the northern end of the Lake, and pass through Capernaum to Bethsaida-Julias.

Beyond the boundaries of Galilee there were several important cities of which the most prosperous were Scythopolis, Gadara, Ptolemais and Caesarea. But there was little urban life to be found in

Galilee outside Sepphoris. The main market cities were outside the district, and the distinction between rich and poor was probably defined almost exclusively in terms of land ownership. By far the largest landowner was Antipas himself, and the fact that Sepphoris, the city of his residence, remained (at least until AD 19/20) the only city worth mentioning, illustrates the centralized, feudal character of his authority.

Antipas was responsible for collecting and paying to Rome the tribute from Galilee and Peraea. Thus all produce and most transactions were subject to tax, and poll and property taxes were also levied. Imported goods became expensive, not only because they were dutiable, but also because merchants had to pay $2\frac{1}{2}\%$ of their value to each city where they kept them overnight on the way to the point of sale. Of the money thus collected Antipas was personally authorized to receive two hundred talents (which amounts to about 70p [$1.30] per head of population).

We have too little information to know what proportion of a family's annual income went in taxation: one scholarly guess is that the amount may have been between 40% and 50%. It is true that the local collectors, or 'publicans' as they were called, were unpopular, but such is the lot of all tax collectors whether or not they are exacting large

11 Benches in the palace at Masada, to accommodate the long queue of subjects who came to seek audience with Herod when he was in residence

sums. The test is perhaps that we know of no complaint or demonstration against the level of taxation required by Antipas, despite the fact that some of the payment went into his private income. What, then, did his subjects expect him to do for them?

Antipas' father, Herod the Great, built himself a palace at Masada, which speaks eloquently of the relationship between rulers of his kind and their subjects, for it contains not one but several waiting rooms equipped with long benches. The ruler was, like the feudal lord, personally available to any of his subjects who wished to consult him. Part of the art of kingship was (and still is in some countries today) knowing how to handle the queue of persons waiting for audience. Many of those who wished to speak to the ruler lived some distance from his residence, and needed to eat at his table and spend the night under his roof if they were to meet him. Antipas therefore knew many of his subjects personally, and was constantly in the position of acting as their host and giving them gifts, small ones to meet the demands of courtesy as well as others which would support his image as a liberal and open-handed lord. This image was further enhanced by the founding of cities, such as Tiberias, and the erection of public buildings, such as its stadium.

Besides acting as arbiter in many of the personal problems and disputes of his subjects Antipas was also expected to relieve them in times of public disaster. We know of no time when he himself had to act in this way, but during the famine of 24 BC his father had readily used his private fortune for relief, 'cutting up into coinage all the gold and silver ornaments in his palace', and, as Josephus informs us, using this money to buy corn in Egypt.

Of the village of Nazareth in Jesus' time we know next to nothing, from either documents or archaeology. Nor are we in any position to know exactly what was implied in Nathanael's contemptuous remark, 'Can any good come out of Nazareth?' (John 1:46). But we know something of the housing of Jesus' time from the Franciscans' excavations in Capernaum, and can gain an idea also of part of the town plan there. In Ill. 12 the general outline is shown of what was revealed by the end of 1972: these houses were built, according to the excavators, in the time of Jesus, and remained in use, doubtless with minor alterations and additions, for about six hundred years. Here, then, are houses Jesus may well have visited. Three centuries later a large room in one of them was held by the local Christians to have been the 'house of Peter'. This room is in the left-hand group of ruins near the foot of the plan (Ill. 12), and is marked with a triangle.

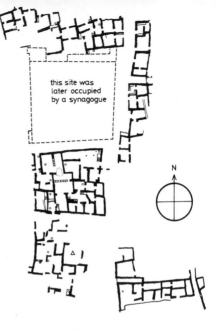

this site was
later occupied
by a synagogue

N

12 Plan of ancient blocks of houses at Capernaum as revealed by the Franciscan fathers in their excavation. They date the building of the houses to the time of Jesus

13 Remains of houses in the block south of the synagogue site at Capernaum. The low windows (arrow) served for ventilation

50 metres

The walls, as appears even from the summary plan given here, were unevenly made of basalt blocks, and were nowhere strong enough to support an upper storey. The various staircases, of which the lower three or four steps have been preserved here and there, must therefore have led on to the roof. Such an arrangement fits precisely the description of the occasion when Jesus was teaching, and four men brought a paralyzed man to see him. The house (as the plan leads us to see) was too crowded with listeners for them to come near him, so they 'removed the roof above Jesus, and when they had made an opening, they let down the bed on which the paralyzed man lay' (Mark II: 3–4). None of the rooms so far revealed have a span of more than 5.5 metres (about 18 feet), probably because of the size of wood or rushes available for roofing. The floors are uneven, being made of large smooth pieces of basalt with sizable cracks between them. Even in the bright sunshine we can imagine the woman in the parable of Luke XV: 8 searching for her lost coin, especially in a room with basalt walls and floor, and small windows. No wonder she had to use a lamp.

14 *There is a coin on this ancient basalt floor at Chorazin, to illustrate the parable in Luke*

15 Looking down one of the streets discovered at ancient Capernaum

Our plan shows also that the ruins to the south of the site later occupied by the synagogue form the east end of a solid block of houses. The part excavated is surrounded by streets or alleys, and seems to comprise four apartments, all giving onto one central court – if we are right in thinking that there was once a door in the area on the north of the court where the ruins are missing (marked by the dotted line). In this part we should therefore picture four families, maybe comprising eight persons each, living in what we can see of this block. Under such conditions there might never be an hour of the day when a person could be alone in a room in one of these houses. Privacy was therefore unknown to many of the people of Capernaum, and even to arrange for a small group to be with him Jesus had to send people away (see Mark V:40). These remains of housing at Capernaum thus confirm the picture in the Gospels, which suggest that for most of the time Jesus was working with groups. The nature of these remains also goes some way towards explaining why Jesus, when he wanted to be alone, often had to go out into the countryside, or the wilderness.

The fishermen of Capernaum were probably prosperous by comparison with the farmers of Galilee, since their wares, fresh and dried fish and fish sauce, were more unusual. But the houses of Capernaum show that their life could hardly be described as luxurious. Partly this was because Capernaum was such a hot place, with days hot and muggy because of the evaporation from the Lake of Galilee, and nights remaining unpleasantly hot for four long months of each year. Partly it was because the houses were cramped in size, crowded in layout, and (because they were built of basalt) unusually dark. There might of course be times during the day when this gloomy interior formed a welcome rest from the glare outside. But at night the weak light of oil lamps can have had little effect. Reading and embroidery and sewing all had to stop. And when eating and drinking, singing and talking were done the only thing left was bed.

Life in Jerusalem

Herod the Great had begun building Caesarea in about 21 BC and probably finished it in about 9 BC. In the same year it was inaugurated as a city, and in AD 6, if not before, took over from Jerusalem the distinction of being the capital of the kingdom. This gradual take-over was doubtless intended by Herod, and implied a diminishing of the power of the high priests and officials of the Jerusalem Temple. Herod, however, disguised his intentions by lavishly reconstructing the Temple between 18 and 10 BC.

In turning our attention to Jerusalem we are therefore examining a city which in Jesus' adult years had lost its civil power. But it remained a city of considerable wealth, and nothing could rob it of its unique importance to religious Jews, and to the nationalists among them. The wealth of the city came partly from its being the place where the world-wide half-shekel tax was sent by all Jewish communities, which provided large capital sums. These, we may suppose, stimulated the local economy. Partly, also, the city gained through its possession of a very large area of countryside. This was described in 152 BC as 'Jerusalem and its environs' (I Maccabees X: 31), and the district (or 'toparchy') was known by the name 'Oreinē' (which most English versions of Luke I: 39 correctly translate 'hill country'). Pliny gives the names of the toparchies which surrounded it, and thus enables us to guess at its size. Since we also know to which of these districts some of the surrounding villages belonged we can produce a rough map along the lines of Ill. 16. This map is on the same scale as Ill. 10: it shows that there was no inland city (except perhaps Hebron) which could compete with Jerusalem in the area of its territory. Those beside the coast, like Ascalon and Gaza with their long-standing autonomy and privileges, were a different matter. We should therefore picture Jerusalem in Judaea, like Sepphoris in Galilee before the foundation of Tiberias, as the largest city for many miles around, and Pliny, indeed, speaks of Jerusalem as, 'by far the most distinguished city not of Judaea only, but of the whole Orient' (*Natural History* 5 : 14). Pliny had no particular axe to grind when speaking of Jerusalem, and is therefore to be taken seriously.

What made Jerusalem so illustrious? Let us first consider its position. The general shape of Judaea and the location of Jerusalem is shown in Ill. 17 (which should be compared with Ill. 5). The city stands on the edge of the substantial central ridge. It is a long mountain about 16 kilometres wide by 100 long (10 miles by 60) whose

16 (left) The toparchies of Judaea in the time of Jesus. The one containing Jerusalem was also known as Oreinē, the 'hill country' of Luke 1 : 39

17 (right) Judaea, with contour lines at 300-metre intervals. Here the bottom of the Rift Valley has sunk more than 300 metres (1000 feet) below the level of the Mediterranean

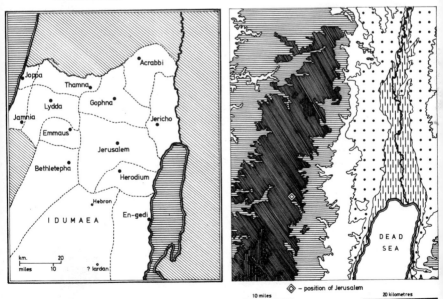

northern and southern limits lie off our map. The ridge runs parallel with the equally substantial Rift Valley, which in the area shown on our map descends farther than 300 metres (about 1000 feet) below the level of the Mediterranean Sea: the whole area below this level is marked on the map by broken vertical shading. The Dead Sea, with its surface at 396 metres (nearly 1,300 feet) below the Mediterranean, and its surrounding area form the lowest exposed place known to exist on the surface of the earth.

The highest points included on our map are nowhere much more than 1,000 metres (about 3,280 feet) above Mediterranean sea level, which means that while the total variation in height that appears on this map is about the same as the variation on Ill. 5, on our map of Galilee, everything is about 200 metres (about 650 feet) lower. We might therefore expect that for Judaea, as for Galilee, the map showing relative heights would also serve as a guide to rainfall. In fact this is not so, not because Judaea is nearer the southern desert, and thus generally hotter and drier than Galilee, but because of the ridge, for which no parallel exists in Galilee. This ridge acts as a rain maker, since the prevailing winds come in from the west and cause the formation of rain clouds on its western slopes. But it also acts as a rain barrier, because, as appears in Ills. 18 and 19, when the clouds are driven eastwards over the watershed they soon disappear. This contrast between cloud formation on the west of the ridge and cloud dispersal on the east leads to contrasts of other kinds as shown in Ill. 20, which shows a variety of conditions around Jerusalem.

On each part of Ill. 20 the position of Jerusalem is shown by a diamond shape. The sectional view (A) cuts through the hills on a line running east and west of the city, which shows the deep Kidron Valley immediately to the east of Jerusalem, and then the Mount of Olives, which is the last high point to the east of the city. From that point the hills roll down eastwards till they end with the cliff-like descent that forms the edge of the Rift Valley about 19 kilometres (12 miles) from Jerusalem, and not shown on our diagram.

Ill. 20B, which shows a strip about 8 kilometres (5 miles) wide corresponding with the section (A), is the rain map of the Jerusalem area. Rain is of critical importance in the Holy Land since it varies between amounts which permit and amounts which prevent the existence of settled life. Thus the general pattern shows a decrease from the west to the east of our strip. Only about 10 kilometres (6 miles) to the east of Jerusalem the rainfall is less than 20 centimetres (8 inches) a year, where ordinary wheat cannot normally grow without irrigation. This area (between Wadi Sidr and Tala'at ed Damm) thus marks the border between the relatively fertile region of Jerusalem and the desert conditions of the lower eastern slopes.

Our soil map, Ill. 20C, provides an interesting reflection of the rainfall pattern. The site of Jerusalem is surrounded by brown soil typical of the Mediterranean, with terra rossa found a little farther west and north. Both of these are soils formed by the simultaneous decomposition of the limestones which underlie them and the vegetable humus produced by prehistoric forests. But the rendzina soils farther to the south and east contain less organic constituents, and the desert soils to the east almost none. The types of soil thus reflect the ancient pattern of vegetable growth, which in turn reflects the rainfall over some very long period. Probably distribution has remained the same since the formation of the ridge shown in Ill. 20A, or in other words for about fifteen million years.

On our soil map the Mediterranean brown and terra rossa are both good for crops, and so is the rendzina, except where it contains too large a proportion of lime. Only the desert soils are not useful. Thus if we compare the rainfall and soil maps we begin to understand where human beings are likely to live. In Ill. 20D the pattern is displayed under yet another guise, this time through the position of the springs in the strip. To the west of Jerusalem there are over thirty springs, but to the east only two. We are thus well prepared for Ill. 20E, which shows the distribution of Arab villages around Jerusalem in 1931 – that is, before the time when military and political factors had made major innovations to the development of the district.

About half the Arab villages shown contained less than 500 people apiece and only Ain Karim (marked with the larger symbol) had more than 3,000.

In the time of Jesus the soil and weather conditions followed the same pattern as that of the present day. On this basis alone we would be safe in assuming that Jerusalem was surrounded by villages with olive and fruit orchards, and that beyond the most easterly villages there was steppe, soon succeeded by desert. In the steppe there are practically no trees, but there is some wheat up to about 8 kilometres (5 miles) east of the city, and sheep and goats can eat the grasses and other growths which are found in the area which stretches 5 or 6 kilometres beyond. Neither in steppe nor desert, however, are there any villages, and the steppe wheat is grown by tent-dwellers ('people-living-the-desert-life' which is the meaning of 'bedouin') as opposed to peasant farmers ('fellahin') with their stone houses.

33

20 (opposite) Conditions around Jerusalem:

A An east–west section through the hills on which Jerusalem stands. The Mount of Olives is immediately to the right (east) of the city. The vertical hatching above the section shows the outline of the hills to the north

B Rainfall in the area through which the east–west section was taken. The area near Jerusalem has about the same rainfall as London (600 mm equals about 24 in.); farther east the rainfall is about the same as Basra in Iraq or el Alamein in Egypt (200 mm equals about 8 in.)

C Soils in the same area. If the mixed soil in the valley beds is discounted there are four types

D Springs in the same area

E The historic villages round Jerusalem in 1931. Newly founded settlements are omitted

18, 19 Clouds regularly disappear as they pass over the Mount of Olives, on the horizon in both pictures, where the ground begins to drop away. Above: looking back at the Mount of Olives from the eastern wilderness. Below: from Jerusalem looking east

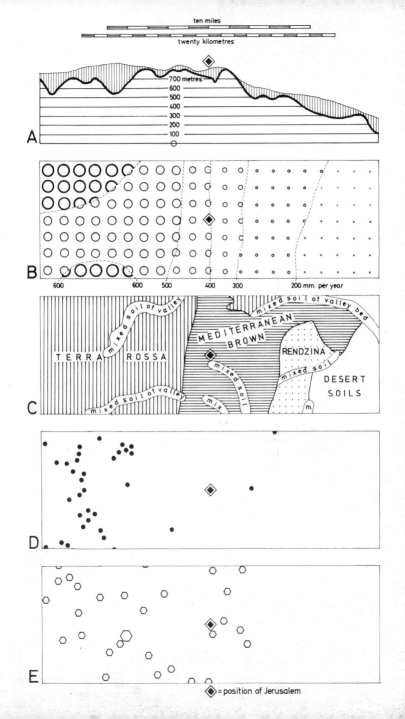

ten miles

twenty kilometres

A

700 metres
600
500
400
300
200
100

B

600   600   500   400   300   200 mm. per year

C

TERRA ROSSA mixed soil of valley MEDITERRANEAN BROWN mixed soil of valley bed RENDZINA mixed soil DESERT SOILS mixed soil of valley mix m.

D

E

◈ = position of Jerusalem

The bedouin live in fine tents made of goats' hair and those who are found in the area shown in our diagrams are semi-nomadic, meaning that they have two camp-sites, one for the winter and one for the summer, and make two moves each year. Whether the winter site is 80 kilometres (50 miles) from the summer one or as little as a quarter of a kilometre, these semi-nomads remain distinct from full nomads, who are constantly on the move.

The boundary between the two life-styles of the fellahin and the bedouin has never been far to the east of Jerusalem, but it would seem, from the ruins in this area, that at certain times in the past the line of occupation by settled farmers extended farther east than it does today. Ruins in the Holy Land are in fact easier to find than those in most parts of northern Europe, since during most periods of history the houses have had to be made of stone due to the scarcity of wood. Thus there have evidently been times when villages stretched farther east than they do now. In interpreting this diagram, Ill. 21 (based on the 1 : 100,000 survey map), it should be remembered that the ruin nearest the top right-hand corner of the diagram was a fort built to guard the lonely stretch of road, and the two to its south-west were monasteries sited in lonely places. These were deliberately placed outside the settled zone.

The frontier between the fellahin and the bedouin no doubt advanced and retreated because of variations in the quantity of rainfall. The averages which we examined in Ill. 20B suppress the variations, since they are based on observations made over a long period. But rainfall can be so irregular that it has serious consequences. Rain usually falls between October and the first half of May, and in the six seasons between 1875 and 1881 the following were annual totals in centimetres: 44.5 – 34.3 – 109.2 – 40.6 – 59.7 – 67.3 (or, in inches: $17\frac{1}{2}$ – $13\frac{1}{2}$ – 43 – 16 – $23\frac{1}{2}$ – $26\frac{1}{2}$). Taking the overall average as 62.5 cm (25 in.) we may deduce that in the first two seasons, with rainfall low, the yield of the crops was poor. The 109 cm (43 in.) which fell in the third season may have caused more harm than good, damaging both the field and terrace walls and perhaps also the crops themselves. Again in the fourth year there was abnormally little rain. Happily this is the most violent set of variations recorded in the past century, but it would be interesting to know how many small farmers failed to survive in the face of this succession of difficult years. Those who were defeated had to abandon their farms and move away, either to some better place outside their home district or perhaps to some other country, to begin again.

21 Distribution of ruins among the villages shown in Ill. 20E

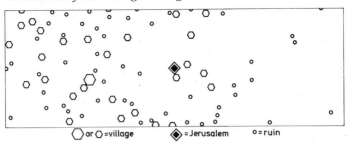

⬡ or ◯ =village   ◈ = Jerusalem   o = ruin

22 Tents of bedouin living in the steppe country 5 kilometres (3 miles) north-east of Jerusalem. The tents are being aired, and the sides are furled up

23 *The tent of a bedouin family living near the limit of wheat cultivation east of Jerusalem*

24 Snow outside Jerusalem's Damascus Gate one February

Conditions as hazardous to farming as these made Judaea a less stable place than Galilee, with its more regular rainfall. Farming anywhere in hill country in the Holy Land is hard, back-breaking work, since there are always so many stones to be picked up. But hard work by itself is not enough to guarantee a good harvest. To the irreligious mind a good harvest also needs good weather, but to the religious it also comes essentially through the favour or displeasure of God. From at least the Chalcolithic Period (about 4000 BC onwards) the concern for fertility is expressed by the making of female figures whose hands are holding their breasts, and such figures are found from all periods thereafter until the middle of the first millennium BC. In literature the same concern is expressed in its most eloquent and comprehensive form in Deuteronomy, Chapter XXVIII, where verses 1–14 deal with blessings and 15–29 with corresponding curses.

With the rest of the places occupying the top of the central ridge, Jerusalem has some cold periods in winter. For four months in each year the mean temperature is less than 15°C (59°F), and in most years there is a light fall of snow. Snow cannot lie long, since there is hardly ever a ground frost. Thus the inhabitants of Jerusalem never experience extreme cold, and only exceptionally extreme heat, for the mean temperature is not expected to rise above 25°C (77°F), nor the maximum above 30°C (86°F). Visitors who experience the maximum heat, which is usually recorded in the first half of the morning before the breeze reaches the city, tend to think of Jerusalem as very hot. But they usually sleep well in the city, because even in midsummer the nights are cool: indeed the highest and lowest temperatures in a summer day and night may vary by as much as 11°C (20°F).

The least pleasant experience Jerusalem has to offer climatically is the condition known in Hebrew as the *sharav* or 'drought' and in Arabic as the *khamsin*, meaning 'fifty', which is perhaps the number of days in the year when it is thought to prevail. High temperatures are accompanied by a sharp drop in humidity, to perhaps half its average, and electrical changes, which make human beings edgy and impatient with each other. Usually the prevailing westerly winds are replaced in these conditions by what Jeremiah calls 'a scorching wind from the high bare places in the wilderness' (Jeremiah IV:11: see also XVIII:17 and Ezekiel XIX:12), and these winds sometimes bring dust from hundreds of kilometres to the east. Here is one of the Deuteronomic curses from Chapter XXVIII:23–24, which describes the misery of the dust storm with its yellow skies: 'And thy heaven that is over thy head shall be brass, and the earth that is under thee shall be iron. The LORD shall make the rain of thy land powder and dust: from heaven shall it come down upon thee till thou be destroyed.'

Jerusalem, at the top of the central ridge, is only 19 kilometres (12 miles) from Jericho on the floor of the Rift Valley. Conditions in Jericho are not unlike those at Capernaum, but since Jericho is 165 kilometres (100 miles) farther south it has more heat: thus high temperatures last roughly twice (and low ones half) as long as they do in Capernaum. The mean temperature in Jericho is over 25°C (77°F) for six months in the year, of which two months have mean temperatures of over 30°C (86°F).

These contrasting conditions, found near Jerusalem as they are in Galilee, are reflected also in the plant and animal life of the area, though the contrasts are more pronounced in Judaea than in Galilee. Analysis of the types of plants that grow in the country between Jerusalem and Jericho shows that they are distributed according to types that link them with four distinct areas in the world around. Round Jerusalem, where there is most rainfall, the plants belong to the flora of the Mediterranean coast, and this zone stretches east as far as the last villages and west, in a visibly similar form, as far as Spain. Both in looks and in life-style Jerusalem may thus be seen as part of the world

25 *Scrub and thorns abound in the rocky steppe country east of Jerusalem, but there are practically no trees*

26 *Four vast climatic areas meet and interlock in the Holy Land. All of them can be detected in the plant and animal life found between Jerusalem and Ein Gedi, a distance of 40 kilometres (25 miles)*

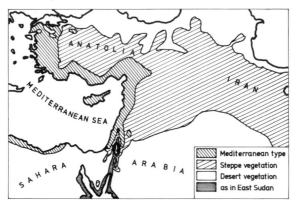

to the west of it. Visitors from that world in Jesus' day would feel at home in the landscape of Jerusalem, and Jerusalemites equally would feel affinities with the countryside of Italy and around Rome.

But the city was only 3 or 4 kilometres from a point where the Mediterranean flora and fauna came to an end. The traveller going east is soon in the treeless steppe, with its plants and animals that are linked with the vast area stretching from Anatolia, the high plateau of central Turkey, over 1500 kilometres (1,000 miles) east into Iran. Jerusalem is therefore a frontier city, never wholly committed to Mediterranean values, and permanently reminded of others. The tensions thus symbolized (and indeed created) were at their height in Jesus' time.

We can see in Ill. 26 that the traveller going a little farther to the south and east of Jerusalem – say to Ein Gedi – passes through a strip of desert whose vegetation and animal life link it with the Sahara to the west and Arabia to the east. To complete this uniquely rich picture we must mention also the characteristic flora and fauna of the floor of the Rift Valley and around Jericho, many elements of which are also to be found in the eastern Sudan. No region of comparable size in the Middle East boasts so wide a variety of climate and environment.

Western Influences

Jews in Judaea in the time of Jesus were in the grip of a cultural conflict. Some, as the New Testament shows, were scrupulous in the observance of their religion. But many were Westernized in their thinking, since they belonged to what was perhaps the tenth generation of Jews influenced by Hellenism. Religiously speaking they were indeed Jews, but in many of their attitudes, ambitions, and assumptions they eagerly accepted the standards of the world about them.

For such Jews, Herod the Great had been the ideal leader. He seems to have had no personal religious commitment, and the synagogues that have been discovered in his castles are evidently additions made by Jewish guerillas seventy years after his death. But Herod valued religion as a means of influence: thus we find that he erected temples to Augustus in Judaea at Sebaste and (surely) at Caesarea, as well as in Phoenicia at Berytus and Tyre. His works included the construction of a large temple at Caesarea Philippi, and the renewal of the Pythian Temple at Rhodes. He ingratiated himself with the Idumaeans – from whom his own family came – by building them sanctuaries at Mamre and Machpelah for their local cult of Abraham, and, as the last of a long series, he erected the Temple for the Jews in Jerusalem. By his deeds he proclaimed that religion was relative rather than absolute. Indeed it is easy to draw comparisons between the periods of Saul, David and Solomon, when the ancient Israelites took the Canaanite culture into their system, and this period of Herod, when Hellenism came to its height among the Jews.

27 Trees in the Kidron Valley east of the Old City of Jerusalem. The olives and cypresses could be seen anywhere around the Mediterranean; the monument is known as the 'Tomb of Absalom'

28, 30 The tomb of the Bene Hezir (right) is certainly, and the 'Tomb of Absalom' (opposite) is probably, a product of the Hellenistic culture among the priestly upper class in Jerusalem in the second century BC

29 (below) The massive stone walls of the sanctuary over the Cave of Machpelah in Hebron, about 32 kilometres (20 miles) from Jerusalem, must have been built by Herod the Great. The parapet with its battlements and the gable on the right are medieval additions

Hellenistic influence was itself nothing new. Everyone knew of the time, at the accession of Antiochus Epiphanes in AD 175, when the high priest had 'wished to abandon his country's laws . . . and adopt the Greek way of life. Accordingly they [namely the High Priest and his followers] asked him [Antiochus] to allow them to build a gymnasium in Jerusalem. They also concealed their circumcision in order to "be Greeks" even when they were unclothed' (Josephus, *Jewish Antiquities* 12:240ff.).

This high priest, whose Semitic name was Onias, also used the Hellenistic name Menelaus, and the use of two such names, often with roughly similar pronunciation, was then and continued to be common amongst the Jews of Judaea. Indeed there are several Jews mentioned in the New Testament only by their Greek names, such as Philip or Nicodemus, though the non-Semitic name was an addition – a

'surname' like John's name Mark (i.e. Marcus) mentioned in Acts XII: 12.

The activity of 'Menelaus' is reported not only by Josephus, but also in I Maccabees I: 11–15 (of which Josephus's words may be an adaptation). It is one of the critical events which led to the Maccabees' campaigns, and to the expulsion of the Seleucids from the Holy Land. But even in an independent Jewish state the dominant Western culture provided forms of expression and activity that were impossible in Semitic languages and social patterns. Hellenism existed as a strong influence among the Jews in Jerusalem as we can see from their monuments. The tomb of the priestly family, the Bene Hezir, for example, and the later 'Tomb of Absalom' near by reflect aspects of Hellenistic architecture. The monuments we know from the period beginning with the construction of the Bene Hezir tomb (about 130 BC) and ending with the destruction of the Jerusalem Temple in AD 70 are the products of one school of thought (and, one may suppose in some cases, of one contracting firm), and we can even identify in such things as the design of column capitals a distinct local style.

The strength of Western influence increased after Pompey's capture of Jerusalem in 63 BC, and from this time onwards rulers of the Jews were all regarded as subject to the imperial authority of Rome. The first major crisis came when the Parthians (i.e. Persians), who led the Eastern bloc, invaded the Holy Land in 40 BC, a move analogous to the USSR invading West Germany today. Mattathias Antigonus, the heir to the royal and high priestly tradition, at once joined the invaders and was recognized by them as Prince of the Jews. But he had underestimated both the strength of Rome and the importance of Judaea in the frontier defences of its empire, and by 37 BC Rome had responded by appointing its own client-prince, Herod the Great, King of the Jews. When Herod had defeated Antigonus, Western influence returned in strength and came to a climax.

The bronze coinage of the Holy Land during this and the next period gives us a fascinating, though sometimes ambiguous, glimpse into the official mind. Gold and silver coins were of course used, but none were struck at this time by the local rulers in the Holy Land. Local gold and silver coins only made their appearance with the next large-scale attempt at Jewish independence in AD 66. Thus the mere fact that any Jew wishing to use gold and silver coins had to use pagan types might act as a reminder of his subjection to Gentiles. Typical coins circulating in the Levant in Jesus' time were the two-drachma pieces minted in Tyre, which performed the function of the US dollar

31 Silver coins used in Jesus' lifetime: (a) Tyre's two drachma piece, (b) a denarius of Augustus minted at Antioch, and (c) an imperial denarius of Tiberius

in our own day, or the imperial four-drachma pieces, or *denarii* like types (b) and (c), Ill. 31. Technically these were likely to be regarded as offensive to strict Jews because the Tyrian two-drachma coin represented the Tyrian god Melkart (by this time 'surnamed' Hercules), the *denarius* of Augustus (b) had on its back the tutelary god of the city of Antioch (where the coin was minted) and its river the Orontes, and the imperial *denarius* of Tiberius (c) displayed a female figure representing the goddess Peace. All these could be construed as idols. But to strike a coin showing even the head of the emperor himself might be taken to constitute disobedience to the Second Commandment, 'Thou shalt not make to thyself any graven image' (Exodus XX : 4). In this context we may note also the paganism of the abbreviated title *pontifex maximus* on the coin of Tiberius (c), which referred to the highest religious honour Rome could bestow, the presidency of the priests who administered religious law.

The sheer convenience of these foreign coins probably dulled religious sensitivities about them. Certainly they were not issued in order to offend the Jews, and the Jews therefore took no offence. But the coins specially produced for use in Jewish population centres took the religion into consideration. Those with which Jesus was familiar probably included a good number which had been struck by Herod the Great, and the three designs of his which are perhaps easiest to explain are those of Ill. 32, the doubled cornucopia (a)–(c), the anchor (d) and the eagle (e). All three had been used before Herod's time. The cornucopia was familiar in Syria as a sign of prosperity, and had been used on Jewish coins before Herod by Alexander Jannaeus (103–76 BC), coin (a), then by Herod (b) and after him by Valerius Gratus, prefect of Judaea under Tiberius from AD 15 to 26 (c). The anchor (d) is shown on a coin inscribed in Greek 'Of King Alexander', that is, Alexander Jannaeus, who used it as one of the royal devices earlier in use by the Seleucids; Herod the Great minted at least seven other types of coin like it, and Archelaus after him at least three. Similarly the eagle (e) which was used by Herod the Great had been used as a royal device by the Ptolemies.

Herod the Great also minted the coins shown in Ill. 33. One clue to his Hellenizing tastes was the language of the inscriptions, which on all his coins was Greek only, and neither Hebrew, nor Hebrew with Greek added. Another clue is that no one looking at Ill. 33 would at once guess that the coins were those of a ruler whose title was 'King of the Jews'. No one is yet quite sure of the identity of the objects shown on coin (b) – it could be a helmet of the type worn by Castor and Pollux – but coin (a) is the winged caduceus, the emblem borne by a carrier of good news, which is so often to be seen in the hand of the herald-god Hermes or Mercury. And if the caduceus has a pagan background so perhaps does the tripod shown by itself on coin (d) and with a bowl resting on it in coin (c). Most likely these are further signs of Herod's Hellenistic tendencies, in this case his fondness for athletic games, for tripods and bowls were commonly given as prizes. It hardly needs saying that such games were, at least to religious Jews, regarded as one of the more offensive pursuits of the Gentile world.

When Jesus used the coins of Herod the Great they spoke to him, in all likelihood, of his parents' generation, when the King of the Jews had ruled large regions to the north, which had contained many Gentiles. But in his own generation that kingdom was split into three, and instead of the title 'king', the Romans permitted only the less honourable 'ethnarch' to Archelaus, who ruled Judaea and Samaria (see Ill. 34, a/c), and the still more junior 'tetrarch' for his brothers Herod Antipas – coins (d) and (e) – and Philip – coins (f) and (g). Archelaus' coins present us with a repertory of types much narrower than that of his father. There are vegetable types (a), and inanimate symbols of armed might like the war galley, such as coin (b), which is

32 Standard devices on bronze coins current in the time of Jesus: cornucopias, issued by (a) Alexander Jannaeus (with a pomegranate in the middle), (b) Herod the Great, and (c) Valerius Gratus (with a caduceus in the middle); royal symbols, (d) anchor, issued by Alexander Jannaeus and also used by Herod the Great, and (e) eagle, issued by Herod the Great

33 Pagan religious devices on the coins of Herod the Great: (a) winged caduceus, (b) perhaps helmet of the Dioscuri, (c) tripod with bowl, (d) tripod

34 The coins of Herod's sons: (a) bunch of grapes, (b) war galley, and (c) helmet – all issued by Archelaus; (d) reed, probably the symbol of Tiberias, and (e) palm branch – both issued by Antipas; (f) portrait of Tiberius, and (g) the temple of Augustus at Paneas – issued by Philip

a   b   c   d

35 Coins of the earlier Roman governors of Judaea: (a) palm tree, and (b) ear of wheat – issued by Ambibulus; (c) palm branch, and (d) vine leaf – issued by Valerius Gratus

a   b   c   d

36 Pagan devices on the coins of Pontius Pilate: of the coins issued by Pilate two carry pagan devices, (a) the simpulum, *or ladle, and (d) the* lituus, *or wand; on (c) both appear; (b–c) the imperial denarius of Augustus*

inscribed with his title in Greek – and the fine helmet with its flowing crest coin (c). Archelaus had to live by (at the very least) two standards, those of Jerusalem and those of Caesarea, and his coins seem to be designed to please people in both cultural environments. Herod Antipas on the other hand was dealing with a population containing a larger proportion of religious Jews, and confined himself to vegetable designs, like the reed or the palm branch as on (d) and (e). Both these coins, and all the others minted by Antipas, consist of a vegetable design on one side and a wreath on the other, which contains an inscription. Philip's coin – (f) is the head and (g) the tail – was intended for circulation in areas north and east of Galilee where the Jewish population was, at least in Philip's time, a minority. Hence he was free to circulate this coin with Tiberius' head on one side and on the other a temple, probably the one which his father, Herod the Great, had built at Philip's capital, Caesarea Paneas, or (as it was known in his reign) Caesarea Philippi.

Archelaus ended his ten years' reign in disgrace and was exiled to Gaul in AD 6, when the Romans assumed direct responsibility for Judaea and Samaria. In Ill. 35 two coins – (a) and (b) – are shown, struck by the procurator Ambibulus in AD 10/11 and two of AD 17 – (c) and (d) – struck by the first prefect Valerius Gratus. All, probably out of delicacy for Jewish feelings in a difficult period, have vegetable designs: palm tree, wheat- (or barley-) ear, palm branch, and vine-leaf. Under Pontius Pilate, however, consideration for Jewish feelings had diminished, as we know from Josephus: Ill. 36 shows two coins – (a) and (d) – struck by Pilate that have the same implements appearing between the two spears and above the shields on the tail side of coin (b)/(c). This coin is an imperial silver *denarius* of Augustus showing his heirs (DESIG. PRINC. IVVENT.) Caius and Lucius Caesar on the back, and Augustus' own portrait on the front. The implements are the *simpulum* (a), which was a ladle for making libations, and the *lituus* (d), the augur's wand. Both – on (c) – are indications of Augustus' dignity as Roman *pontifex maximus*. Either symbol, on Pilate's coins, was likely to offend the religious Jews who recognized the pagan implications.

The City Plan

These coins point to Herod the Great as the greatest Hellenizer in the century before Jesus' death and resurrection, and this suggestion gains considerable strength through recent archaeological discoveries in the Jewish Quarter of the Old City of Jerusalem, which enable us to form a definite notion of the type of city plan that Jesus must have known there, and a working hypothesis about its precise layout.

Today's 'Old City' of Jerusalem, the area surrounded by the

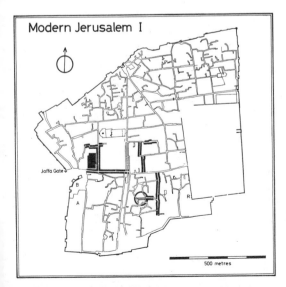

37 Some Herodian elements in modern Jerusalem. Besides the marked streets and the so-called 'Hezekiah's Pool', note that R is 'Robinson's Arch', the top of a great staircase; A is the site of Herod's Palace; and B the site of the present-day Citadel

sixteenth-century walls, overlaps the area of the walled city of the period of Herod the Great. In the site marked by a circle on Ill. 37 Professor Nahman Avigad dug trenches that revealed the foundations of a street, and beneath it the remains of a house that had been occupied early in Herod's reign (he was King from 37 BC to 4 BC), and then demolished. Although the curb of the street was not discovered, Avigad located the foundations over a length of about 50 metres (55 yards), and they certainly run in the direction of 'Robinson's Arch' (marked R on the wall of the Haram esh Sharif). The foundations of the ancient street join one in use today which more or less continues its line towards the arch. On Ill. 37 we have marked the edges of this and some of the other modern streets with a thickened line.

If we turn to Josephus we find him reporting the monuments, forts, palace, and Temple built by Herod the Great. But Avigad's discovery shows something more, for Herod must have evicted the family living in the house in order to lay the foundations of the new street, and it seems likely that if he laid one street he was probably setting out a new system. Capernaum has given us an example of town layout where a grid of streets defines the edges of the residential building blocks or 'islands' as they were called, and we know how in sophisticated cities like Damascus or Laodicea there was, from Hellenistic times, a grid layout of streets covering the whole city area. So we may well find such a grid in Jerusalem.

Clearly not all the streets in present-day Jerusalem are to be dated to the time of Herod the Great. Thus Ill. 37 gives the strong impression that the north-south streets to the west (left) of Avigad's excavation were at one stage parallel with each other. But they are certainly not parallel with the marked north-south street to the east (right) of the excavation, and to the present writer they seem to have been realigned about a century after Jesus' death and resurrection, in the time of Hadrian. But there are some other phenomena which may reflect another and earlier grid pattern. Thus if the street to the east of the remains found by Avigad was of the same date and at right angles, and if both formed part of a grid, we may note that the marked streets slightly to the north look as though they could have belonged to the same system. Furthermore the alignment of David Street (leading towards the western gate of the city) and of the so-called 'Hezekiah's Pool', shown in solid black just to the north, seem to fit such a grid very well.

If there was a grid, what determined its direction? We must ask what works are likely to have taken place in this part of the city after

Herod's succession in 37 BC that might have formed the starting-point for the eviction of householders and the creation of a new street layout. Of all the works mentioned by Josephus the one that seems most likely to have had these consequences is the palace Herod built when he was fifty years old. Its site covered the present police barracks and Armenian garden (marked A on Ill. 37: compare Ill. 38) and extended north to include the three towers Phasael, Hippicus, and Mariamme, which probably fell within the area of the present Citadel (B). A possible alternative position for these three towers is shown on Ill. 37. They are discussed at greater length below (see p. 140).

38 The site of the Palace of Herod the Great seen from the south. It covered roughly the area shown between the two arrows. The present Citadel is at the top. The large tower on the extreme right of the present Citadel is probably identical in its lower part with Herod's tower named Phasael

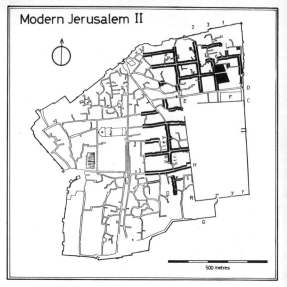

39 Some Herodian streets round the Temple enclosure: (C) the 'false corner', (D) St Stephen's Gate, (E) site of the fort Antonia, (F) the Pool of Israel, (G) part of the Turkish city wall, and (H) the Gate of the Chain, directly above 'Wilson's Arch'. Streets on the lines 1–1′, 2–2′, and 3–3′ lead respectively in the directions of the Single, Double, and Triple Gates in the south wall of the Temple enclosure

The actual buildings of Herod's Palace have left no recognizable trace, apart from the base of one of the towers. But now that some excavations have been carried out in the Citadel and the Armenian Garden we have learned that the buildings were artificially raised on an immense plinth 3 metres (10 feet) high and at least 60 metres (196 feet) wide and 300 metres (982 feet) long. Such a large earthwork would in itself be a determining factor in the layout of the neighbouring streets, and we shall here assume that they were aligned with it, though in the present state of the evidence we cannot yet be finally sure.

Herod reached the age of fifty in 23 BC. During this year he built not only his Palace in Jerusalem but a second fortified palace as well (to serve also as his tomb), near Bethlehem, which he named the Herodium. It seems probable that in the same year he was also making a channel 45 kilometres (28 miles) in length to augment the city water supply. This sudden large-scale campaign of construction work most likely was a relief programme specially mounted to relieve the hardships caused by the famine of the previous season, 25/24 BC.

The new Temple, which Herod began to build in 19 or 18 BC, was a monument even greater than the Palace. Judging from the modern streets marked on Ill. 39 the Temple also formed the base for a rectangular grid of streets, which is considerably clearer and more extensive than the one we have supposed as existing around the Palace. In order to form the origin of a rectangular street grid we should

40 *The north side of the 'false corner' seen from the north*

41 *The 'false corner', corresponding with the north-east corner formed by the joining of the east and present north walls of the Haram esh Sharif. Though constructed in stones doubtless cut in the time of Herod the Great, the corner exists above ground only and is not matched by any corresponding corner in the Herodian wall below*

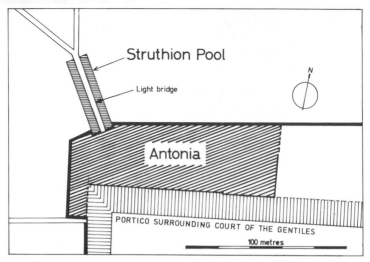

Struthion Pool

Light bridge

N

Antonia

PORTICO SURROUNDING COURT OF THE GENTILES

100 metres

42 The relation of the rock plinth that supported the fort Antonia and the Struthion Pool. The unexpected angle of the pool may be a result of its having been constructed to serve the Baris, a building of Hyrcanus I that was replaced by the Antonia

43 The north end of the Haram esh Sharif seen from the south. The rock plinth beneath the Umariya School (the site of the Antonia) is just visible (arrow) behind the trees

44 The Struthion Pool has, since the time of Hadrian (AD 135), been hidden beneath a pavement: this is one of the two barrel-vaults over the pool, which now support the pavement. Until AD 70 the pool was open

expect the exterior of the Temple's enclosure wall to be rectangular, and this is hard to envisage so long as we are considering the interior of the present Haram esh Sharif as simply surrounded by a wall. But Herod's outer wall 'included the Tower Antonia' according to Josephus (*War* 5:192), which means that the outer wall of his time probably coincided not with the present inner wall leading to the false corner (C), but with the line of the present street which leads to the gate marked (D) on Ill. 39. At any rate this present-day street can hardly have been a street before AD 70, since in that year Josephus tells us that the Fifth Legion attacked the Antonia 'across the middle of the pool called Struthion' (*War* 5:467 – *struthion* is Greek for 'swallow'). Thus the pool was not yet covered by stone vaults as it is now, and the present street cannot have passed over it as it does now. At first sight it seems highly improbable that soldiers should choose to attack by building earthworks across the middle of a pool. But the easiest solution of the apparent difficulty is to assume that the legion was seeking to reach the weakest point in the defences, namely the gate by which people normally entered the castle from the outside. Heavy shading in Ill. 42 shows the 9 metre (about 30 feet) rock plinth on which the castle was built and the pool, and shows how the normal access to the gate was probably by a drawbridge.

This door at the north-west corner of the Antonia was thus the north-west corner also of the outer walls of the Temple area, while the north-west corner of the inner walls of the enclosure – or Court of the Gentiles – was at the end of the wall leading from point (C) on Ill. 39.

45 Sketch-plan of the ancient layout of the area west of St Anne's Church. The street leading into the city from St Stephen's Gate probably corresponds with the line of the outer north wall of Herod's Temple enclosure

46 Looking west into the city from St Stephen's Gate. St Anne's Church is the white-roofed building with the small dome to the right of the Gate, and the excavations of the Sheep-pool (or Pool of Bethesda) lie under the trees (arrows) beyond the church

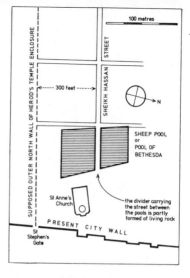

Between the inner and outer walls of the enclosure lay what appears to have been a 'utilities area' containing the Antonia (E) and the pool called the Pool of Israel (F). Confirmation of this externally rectangular shape for the Temple area seems to be provided by the Pools of Bethesda, which are divided by a causeway of living rock (compare Ill. 45 and Ill. 46), which is the right width to have carried a street, and from which today a street indeed extends westwards into the city. This street is precisely 91 metres (300 feet) from our supposed outer north wall of the Temple area and thus matches the existing Valley Street (Tariq el Wad), which is 91 metres from the western wall. Probably the Turkish city wall at (G) on Ill. 39, which is 91 metres from the south wall of the Temple area, also recalls the line of one of the streets which framed Herod's Temple area.

How can we be sure of the date of this frame of streets round the Temple area? Was not Jerusalem destroyed by Titus and radically transformed by Hadrian? We are told so by ancient authors, but we are told the same about other ancient cities, such as Corinth, where we know that much of the city reported to have been destroyed is still recoverable. We are encouraged to think the same for Jerusalem because the intervals between the streets running north from the Temple area towards the numbers 2, 3, and 1 (Ill. 39) appear to correspond with those between the gates in the south wall of the area,

47 Fine paving that was laid by Herod the Great as part of the rearrangement of the streets immediately round the Temple enclosure: Jesus is very likely to have walked on it. The large stones lying on it formed part of the wall of the enclosure, and were thrown down to the paving in AD 70

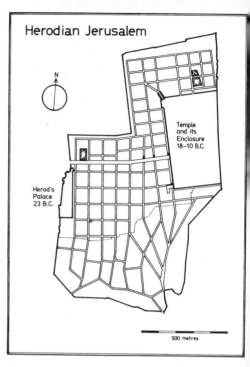

Herodian Jerusalem

N

Temple and its Enclosure 18–10 B.C.

Herod's Palace 23 B.C.

500 metres

48 A restoration of the street layout of Jerusalem as completed by Herod the Great. Many details are necessarily based on guesswork but there is every probability that there were gridded streets

49 Ancient stepped street climbing the slopes of Jerusalem's western hill. This long stretch is visible in the grounds of the Church of St Peter in Gallicantu

the Single (1′), Double (2′), and Triple (3′) Gates, of which the latter two are certainly Herodian in position. We are also likely to find that the excavated shape of the Bethesda Pools goes back to the time of Herod the Great.

Let us therefore suppose that Herod the Great laid out two street grids for Jerusalem, one, connected with his construction of the Palace in 23 BC, in the west of the city; and the other, laid out around the walls of the Temple enclosure, connected with the work of construction which lasted from 19 or 18 BC. Being slightly different in orientation, the two grids may have joined in a somewhat irregular way (as is suggested by the lines of some of the present streets). The streets known to Jesus in Jerusalem would therefore have been like those set out in Ill. 48. In the area to the north of the present south wall (marked by the dotted line) the streets are laid out in a grid pattern, but south of that line the slopes are mostly too steep for a grid, and any ancient streets that have so far been found either run horizontally (following the contour lines) or take the form of stepped streets taking the most direct way up the slopes.

Most discussions of Herod's Jerusalem have begun with an examination of what Josephus tells us about the city walls. This is no easy undertaking, since the passage concerned contains so many unknown reference points, and also because of Josephus' age. He was born in about AD 37, which meant that he was just too young to have any clear personal memories of the line of the walls before the time of Herod Agrippa's alterations in AD 44. Unfortunately we are unable to add very much to Josephus' account through archaeological discovery, for though the line of the outer southern wall is undoubted, it has not yet been dated. Indeed, the only section of wall on which Josephus and the archaeologists now agree is that part on the west of the palace, spared by Titus (*War* 7:2*ff.*), which, it has now been discovered, has foundations going back to the period before Herod the Great.

Here is what Josephus tells us in *War* 5:142–45, with comments:

The oldest of three walls . . . began at the north at the tower called Hippicus [certainly near the position marked on Ill. 50]. It extended to the Xystus [not known but see pp. 86–87] and then, joining the Council Chamber [not known], ended at the western portico of the Temple.

[From Hippicus] on the west going in the other direction it stretches through the area called Bethso [not known] to the Gate of

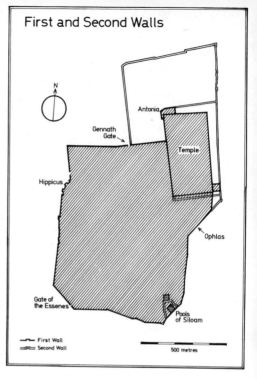

First and Second Walls

Antonia

Gennath Gate

Temple

Hippicus

Ophlas

Gate of the Essenes

Pools of Siloam

—•— First Wall
═▨═ Second Wall

500 metres

50 The 'First and Second' walls of Jerusalem as described by Josephus do not seem to fit the archaeological data. Possibly they were more like what is suggested here

the Essenes [not known, but there was a gate at the point tentatively indicated].

Then on the south it turned above the Siloam spring to run on the east towards Solomon's Pool [not known] and, passing on as far as a place called Ophlas [certainly near the position marked] joined the eastern portico of the Temple.

In *War* 1:401 Josephus says that Herod 'restored the Temple and, by building new foundation walls, enlarged the surrounding area to double its former extent'. He also tells us in *War* 5:146 that: 'The Second Wall started at the gate in the First Wall called Gennath [not known] and, enclosing only the northern district of the town, went up as far as the Antonia.'

If our understanding of the streets is correct then it looks as if Josephus might be wrong here, for we envisage Herod the Great as extending the street system to stretch beyond the Antonia both on the north and on the east in order to include what was known in Greek as Kainopolis (New City) and in Aramaic as Bethesda. Josephus on the other hand goes on in *War* 5 : 147 apparently to imply that this area was not enclosed till after Jesus' death and resurrection, by the efforts of Herod Agrippa.

The Jerusalem Jesus knew, therefore, displayed a fashionable and sophisticated city plan. It stood in sharp contrast with the hamlet of Nazareth and the country town of Capernaum, and its monumental engineering and architecture were all the more impressive since they were less than fifty years old in Jesus' lifetime.

The Population

It is hard to conceive the Jerusalem of Jesus' time without some Gentile inhabitants. There were surely foreigners acting in the theatre, conducting businesses, organizing events in the hippodrome, and serving at court in the bodyguard of the ethnarch. After the exile of Archelaus in A D 6 the number of foreigners in the city was augmented by the presence of foreign auxiliary units of the Roman army. The city was nevertheless almost exclusively Jewish, and we should probably picture the foreigners as mainly specialists.

Among the Jews the variety was immense. Jews 'from every nation under heaven' assembled for the feasts, and some of them stayed on in the city as residents. Amongst them it was possible, no doubt, to find every degree of religious commitment, and there must have been a good many who were so wedded to Hellenistic ways that they were hardly Jews at all in the sense of being persons who practised the Jewish religious way of life by keeping the Law.

Jerusalem was thus a predominantly Jewish city, but its special character came from the fact that its Temple was not only of local interest, but belonged to every Jew in the world. Certain Jewish religious acts could be performed only in the Temple at Jerusalem, and the Jerusalem Council, the 'Sanhedrin', was the only central reference point for the interpretation of religious law. It is ironic that even this body should have been called by a Greek name, for 'Sanhedrin' is simply a rendering of *synedrion*, Greek for council.

This central status of Jerusalem for international Jewry had its financial corollary. Unlike any of the cities in Syria it received annual Temple dues from a large and organized 'Dispersion', and consequently, again unlike the cities which were around it, it received immense amounts of cash. It is most unlikely that this cash was simply held in safe keeping in the Temple vaults. The Temple must surely have served as a bank, and put the cash back into circulation by lending, and financing businesses. Indeed, we learn from Josephus that Pilate caused a disturbance by 'spending the sacred fund called Corbonas on a water-supply' (*War* 2:175). Something about Pilate's action provoked a popular demonstration against him. But the complaint seems not to have been that he had somehow managed to obtain money given to the Temple authorities, but that he had received money from the wrong fund.

As the prosperity of Jerusalem attracted more and more people their presence created a problem, for Jerusalem is, as we have seen, sited on top of the central ridge of the country, and only has access to limited amounts of water. Though we cannot date the ancient systems with precision we may envisage the reign of Herod the Great as a time when a great deal of water would be needed for an increasing number of citizens, and still more for public and royal use (such as feeding the canals and ponds in Herod's Palace). We may therefore envisage, during Herod's reign, a much more widespread system of exploiting water resources. The kind of alteration involved is illustrated by Ills. 51 and 52, which show not only rain-collecting pools, but also the low-level aqueduct coming from Etam. It is very probable that Herod extended this aqueduct to draw a more distant supply of water at the same time as he was building his Palace. At any rate he added to the existing aqueduct a section more than twice as long again, extending it from 22.5 to 67 kilometres (14 to 42 miles). The effect was almost to double the amount of water reaching Jerusalem through the aqueduct. We may also guess that in Herod's time more pools were constructed for the collection and distribution of the rainfall in the surrounding catchment areas. This increased supply probably doubled the population ceiling of Jerusalem, say from 35,000 to 70,000, over the reign of Herod the Great. In the light of this sort of figure (which is based on a great many guesses) we may better estimate the strength of the movements presented to us by Josephus as the 'Four Philosophies' of the Jewish people: the familiar Sadducees and Pharisees and the less familiar Essenes and followers of Judas the Galilean (see *War* 2:118 *ff.*, and *Antiquities* 18:11 *ff.*).

There were over 4,000 members of the Essene movement and 6,000 Pharisees, so Josephus tells us. They were therefore small movements, both originating in reactions against a religious establishment. The followers of Judas the Galilean seem simply to have been Pharisees with a nationalistic urge. They organized a revolt against the first of the Roman procurators, Coponius, between A D 6 and 9, and formed the rallying-point for those who later, under the name of 'Zealots', organized and carried out the warfare against Rome which began in

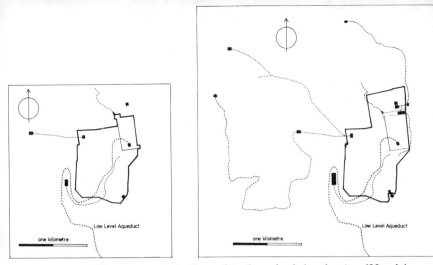

51, 52 Water systems probably supplying Jerusalem before the reign of Herod the Great, and the expanded Jerusalem water supply system as it most likely was after its development by Herod the Great

AD 66 and ended with the siege of Masada in AD 73. Until about 76 BC the establishment had been represented by the hereditary nobility of priests and lay persons who formed the party known as Sadducees. Their privileges could in some cases be traced back as far as the late sixth century BC (such as the right to provide wood for the altar fire: see Nehemiah X: 34–37). But from 76 BC, when Queen Alexandra began her reign, the Pharisees gained increasing influence; and by the time of Jesus the Sadducees were the conservative party within the establishment, opposing not only the Pharisees but also those who, like the followers of Judas the Galilean, were ready to countenance the overthrow of law and order to achieve independence from Rome. During those years that are thought to span the lifetime of Jesus the influential and lucrative office of chief priest was held by members of a single family of Sadducees. But they had lost the leadership in thought to their rivals. Their doctrinal position is distinguished by their refusal to acknowledge an oral as well as a written law, or to admit belief in a resurrection, and by their stand over determinism and free will.

In reaction to the secularism, which came through Gentile and Hellenistic influence, various observant religious groups had come into being in the second century BC, among them the Hasidim (of whom we know very little) and the Pharisees, who may have been

67

associated with Hasidim or indeed identical with them. Pharisees emphasized the need for a scrupulous and complete observance of the Law both in its written form and in the interpretations which had become traditional in the discussions among scholars. In the century of their origin they had represented a valuable force for revival in Judaism, somewhat like the force of Methodism in the British Christianity of the eighteenth century. But the movement was already nearly two centuries old in the time of Jesus and had become part of the establishment. He seems to criticize its members for losing their sense of proportion – for 'straining out a gnat and swallowing a camel' (Matthew XXIII:24). While they remained convinced of the value of the Temple and its worship they objected to the stranglehold on official religion by the Sadducees.

Essenes were a second movement concerned with what they called 'the exact interpretation of the Law', and Josephus gives a longish description of their way of life, having himself undergone the studies and ascetic exercises that were required for membership. Pliny tells us of Essenes who lived by the shore of the Dead Sea, and he marvels at their celibacy. These, it seems certain, included the Qumran community whose Dead Sea Scrolls were discovered thirty years ago, even though the content of the Scrolls and these descriptions of Essenes do not agree in every respect. The Qumran sect distinguished itself both from Pharisees and, for that matter, from the earliest Christians, by renouncing Temple worship under the 'Wicked Priest' Jonathan (high priest 152–143 BC) and setting up a separate community to follow a way of life which would continue in faithfulness to God's Law. Though the community occupied the 'monastery' at Qumran during the adult life of John Baptist and of Jesus (see Ill. 53) we have no direct evidence of any communication with them, and Jesus' attitude to the Temple seems to exclude the possibility that he was in any way closely connected with the doctrines of this small sectarian group.

Jerusalem in the time of Jesus thus formed the pivotal point of Jewish identity and religion. In no other city of that day were Jewish religious and political movements so likely to have effect, but in no other city were the tenacious conservatisms of the Jewish faith present in such strength.

53 (opposite) The monastery at Qumran and the shore of the Dead Sea, looking south-east

Jesus comes to Jerusalem

In the Temple

When the Jews told Jesus that the Temple took forty-six years to build (John II:20) they probably meant that builders had already been at work there for forty-six years. Herod the Great, who had started the works in 20–18 BC, had been able to dedicate the Temple in 10 BC. But that did not mean that all the work was finished, for Josephus tells us that there were 18,000 builders in service there still in AD 63, the date when he regards the Temple as finished and when the labour force was finally dismissed (*Antiquities* 20:220). It is hard to believe that a force of this size was in service continuously for eighty years, but not so difficult to imagine successive benefactors making successive additions during the period.

The Temple area was called Har ha Bayit, 'the Mountain of the House', and was in fact a mountain, though rather a small one. Herod the Great enlarged it by constructing a vast platform around it, and the summit is still visible within the Dome of the Rock. In Jesus' time this summit (if our proposed reconstruction is correct) supported the Altar of Sacrifice. On the east, south, and west the natural slopes of the ground were hidden by Herod's platform, which was doubtless raised on stone vaults. Those that are visible today beneath the south-eastern part of the platform, and known as 'Solomon's Stables', are probably very like the vaults constructed by Herod. Indeed, the stones with which they were assembled were mostly hewn by Herod's masons. But the vaulting as we now know it seems in fact to belong to the Umayyad rebuilding in the seventh and eighth centuries.

The plan of the whole enclosure seen from the east is shown in Ill. 54, and Ill. 56 shows traces of the steps that appear at the left-hand end

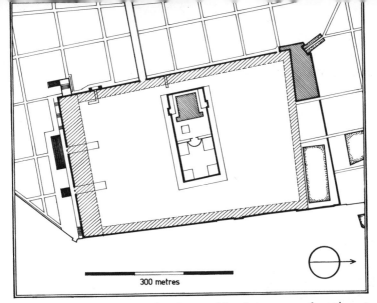

300 metres

54 Plan of the reconstructed Temple area of Jesus' time as seen from the east

55 The vaults beneath the south-east corner of the platform of the Haram esh Sharif, usually known as 'Solomon's Stables'. Comparable vaults must have existed to support the floor of the Temple platform built by Herod the Great

56 The Haram esh Sharif seen from the south-west. The steep banks outside the wall of the Herodian platform rise to their summit beneath the Dome of the Rock

57 The basic elements of the ceiling design in the 'Double Gate'

58 Inside the circle of the dome the squares are arranged in an eight-pointed star. Notice the frequent occurrence of rosettes and the way in which the vines are arranged to fill all the available spaces

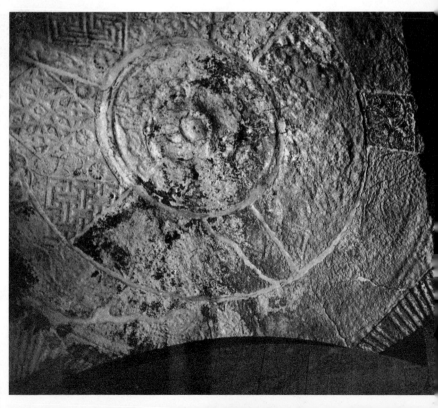

59 Another ceiling design restored from a fragment discovered near the south wall of the Haram esh Sharif by Professor Mazar. This design with its geometric ornament and rosettes forms a 'flower' of interlocking hexagons inside the circle of the dome. Its similarities of style show that the ceiling inside the 'Double Gate' is also part of the Herodian ornament of the Temple enclosure

of the plan. These led up to a pathway along the south wall of the enclosure, which provided access to the two ramps that were entered by the Huldah Gates. These ramps began at the top of the steps and led up to the surface of the raised platform inside. One of these ramps still survives, the one to the west, and its lower entry, the 'Double Gate', is almost exactly beneath the small silver dome of el Aqsa mosque, though most if it is hidden by masonry of a later period. Although what can be seen of it from the outside appears to be Umayyad work, there is a ceiling inside that is surely Herodian, since its design so closely resembles that of other masonry known to be Herodian, as appears from a comparison between Ill. 57 (the design of the ceiling) and Ill. 59 (masonry recently found near the south wall of the Temple enclosure). The most probable reason for having two ramps was to separate the entry from the exit so that those coming in, defiled by the outside world, could be kept from contact with those who had been purified by their visit to the Temple and wished to go out. Possibly the Mishnah implies this sort of arrangement when it says that the two Huldah gates 'served for coming in and for going out' (*Middoth* 1:3) and that normally 'whoever it was that entered the Temple Mount came in on the right and went round and came out on the left' (*Middoth* 2:2). The same effect would be obtained today by notices saying 'Keep to the Right'.

The two ramps led up under the largest of the porticoes surrounding the enclosure. This was known as the 'Royal Portico', and its 162 columns formed three aisles which stretched across the south end of the enclosure from east to west. The middle aisle, according to Josephus, was over 13 metres (45 feet) wide and 30 metres (100 feet) high (*Antiquities* 15:415). The colonnade along the east side of the enclosure, which was smaller, was called 'Solomon's Porch', but we hear of no special names for the other two. From the west end of the middle aisle of the Royal Portico a door opened onto a staircase, which spanned a street as it descended to the west, then turned at right angles to descend to the ground running south. In Ill. 61 we see the beginning of 'Robinson's Arch', which spanned the street; and in Ill. 62 a line of white stones in the sunlight facing the arch, 12 metres (40 feet) from the wall, is in fact the lintels of four small shops built inside the arch. The air photograph shows how in 1975 Professor Mazar's excavation ended at the earth ramp leading up to the modern Gate of the Moors. Beneath this Gate, in a chamber that is inside the ramp, is the lintel of 'Barclay's Gate'. This too is a Herodian entrance to the Temple area and was approached by short flights of steps leading from the street up to a small platform. North of this modern ramp is the section of the wall now specially sacred to Jews and called the 'Wailing Wall' or, more usually, the 'Western Wall'. The space in front is full of worshippers, and beyond it stand medieval Muslim buildings which mask the great arch that formed the first span of a bridge. This arch, 'Wilson's Arch', is all that is identifiable of the masonry of the bridge, but Ill. 64 shows how a line of high buildings stretches across the valley to the west of what used to be the Temple enclosure, and the bridge, or some successor to it, probably provides the foundations for these houses. To the north of the bridge 'Warren's Gate' gives access from ground level to the platform.

The wall itself was not smooth, as much of it seems to be today. It was made of masonry 'drafted', or marked, with a characteristic margin, of which much remains in position. Thus most of the south-east corner shown in Ill. 60, though weathered, is as Herod built it, and as can be seen from the 2-metre stick the bonding stones are of great length. Josephus speaks of Herodian stones that were 75 feet (23 metres) long, and says that the blocks of which the Temple were made were 42 feet (13 metres) in length. This type of masonry in itself may have prompted the disciples to say to Jesus 'Look, Teacher, what wonderful stones and what wonderful buildings' (Mark XIII: 1).

60 (*opposite*) *Massive Herodian masonry still in place in the south-east corner of the Haram esh Sharif. The stick on the right is two metres*

61 (opposite above) 'Robinson's Arch' (arrow) projects from the wall, to the left of the south-west corner of the Haram esh Sharif. It supported a large staircase leading out of the Royal Portico as it crossed the street below, then turned at a right angle, towards the right of our picture, for the lower flight, which descended to ground level

62 (opposite below) The south-west corner of the Haram esh Sharif seen from above. Parallel with the wall in shadow is a line of white masonry (arrow) in the sunlight. This shows that the original span of 'Robinson's Arch' was 12 metres (about 40 feet)

63 (above) Looking south under 'Wilson's Arch'. Herod made this as the first bay of a bridge carrying a street 15 metres (50 feet) wide across from the Temple enclosure to the Upper City

64 (overleaf) The Haram esh Sharif seen from the north. To the right at the far end is a row of high buildings (arrow) with their near side in deep shadow. They contain whatever may remain of the bridge that Herod the Great built across the city's central valley

65 The wide capital (arrow) on the south-west corner of the Golden Gate is assembled from two capitals that are probably Herodian

66 (opposite) The Arab capitals incorporated inside the Gate are executed in a flatter style

Besides the light and shadow created by this carefully finished masonry, the solidity of the enclosure was emphasized by pilasters which surrounded its upper part. Remains of them have been found in Professor Mazar's excavation, and we have in Hebron an identical treatment of the wall surrounding the Haram el Khalil or Shrine of Machpelah. No doubt the pilasters were crowned with acanthus-leaf capitals like those preserved outside the Golden Gate.

The enclosure thus reveals Herod's liking for the Hellenistic style. What of the Temple inside? The one early likeness of it we possess is clearly evidence that the style of the main sanctuary was also Hellenistic. This coin shows a façade with four columns supporting what is probably a flat roof. Above the roof is a star (which shows more clearly on other examples of this coin), but since on some other versions of the coin it is replaced by a wavy line the star is unlikely to belong to the building. Beneath the façade is a motif like a ladder, which is probably a formal representation of one of the porticoes near the main building, and between the inner columns is a round-topped chest seen end on. The two spots halfway up represent the ends of carrying poles, and this is the Ark of the Covenant (see Exodus XXV: 10–16), an object which was lost in 587 BC. The formal rendering of the portico and the symbolic ark are warnings that we are

67 Coin of Simeon Bar Cochba showing the Jewish Temple as it was remembered sixty-five years after its destruction

not necessarily to interpret the façade in an entirely literal manner. On the other hand the coin, made in the third year of Simeon Bar Cochba – in A D 134–5 – must reflect the appearance of the Temple in some general way, even though its designer is hardly likely to have seen the building, which had finally been destroyed sixty-five years before.

Meagre and uncertain as it is, the evidence of the coin certainly adds usefully to what we know about the Temple from detailed literary descriptions provided by Josephus (*War* 5:184–247) and the supplementary information in the Mishnah tractate *Middoth*, which purports to give the measurements of the Temple.

These descriptions and other passing references by Josephus, who saw and knew the building, are not entirely consistent with those of the Mishnah, whose compilers were trying to preserve traditions about the Temple, which were already second- or third-hand. Over many details we remain confused, but there is enough agreement to enable us to reconstruct the overall layout of the Temple with confidence, and any one who compares the different reconstructions that have been proposed will be struck by their consistency. We may thus reasonably hope that Ill. 68 is a good approximation.

On the south, north, and east the inner Temple complex was surrounded by a fence 'three cubits high', marked by the letter P

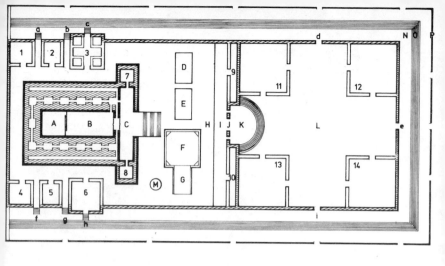

68 *Plan of Herod's Temple as described by Josephus and the compilers of the Mishnah. Many of the details are not known in entirety and many of the following identifications are necessarily conjectural*

*A Holy of Holies (*Debir*)*
*B Holy Place (*Hekal*)*
*C Porch (*Olam*)*
D, E Slaughtering places
F Altar
G Ramp
H East part, Court of the Priests
I Court of the Israelites
J Nicanor ('Beautiful'?) Gate
K Where the Levites stood to sing
L Court of the Women
M Laver
N Terrace
O Fourteen steps
P Barrier

a Gate of the Flame (or Jeconiah)
b Gate of the Offering
c unknown
d Gate of the Women?
e Gate of Singing?
f Kindling Gate
g Firstlings' Gate
h Water Gate
i unknown

1 Salt chamber
2 Parwah ('indeterminate') chamber
3 Chamber of the hearth
4 Wood chamber
5 Golah (cistern) chamber
6 Chamber of hewn stone (beneath chamber of Abtinas)
7, 8 Chambers of the slaughter knives
9 Bakers' chambers
10 Chamber of the Custodian of the Robes
11 Lepers' chambers
12 Wood store
13 Oil store, also for wine
14 Nazirites' chamber

on Ill. 68. We cannot be entirely certain what length Josephus means to indicate by the word 'cubit', but assume that it was 55 centimetres (21½ inches). This fence would thus have been 165 centimetres (over 5 feet) high. It had thirteen gates, and at each was a notice in Latin or Greek, like the one shown in Ill. 69 which read: 'No Gentile to enter the fence and barrier round the Temple. Anyone caught is answerable to himself for the ensuing death.' Ephesians II: 14 calls this fence 'the middle wall of partition'.

The Jewish pilgrim, when he had passed through one of these gates into the Court of the Israelites, mounted fourteen steps and reached the Rampart, a terrace surrounding the wall of the Temple court proper. Lay men and women ordinarily entered through one of the eastern gates (d, e, or i) leading into the Court of the Women. This court (L) was a cruciform space surrounded by four chambers, and the space in front of its west gate represented the farthest point to which women could penetrate. But lay men with a sacrifice to offer

69 Fragment of the inscription on the gates leading from the Court of the Gentiles into the Court of the Israelites. Only the Greek versions have so far been found

85

were permitted to go on through this gate, the Nicanor Gate, or 'Gate Beautiful' (J) and as far as the cubit-high step (or barrier) which marked the division between the Court of the Israelites (I) and the Court of the Priests (H).

In front of the man whose sacrifice was to be offered (and probably also slightly to his left, as suggested on our plan) was the great Altar (F), about 14 metres square and 7 metres high (50 feet square, 25 high). Beyond it was the Laver (M), the immense bronze basin in which the priests purified their hands and feet, and from which on occasion they drew water for other ritual purposes. To the right were the tables, pillars, and hooks for use in the slaughtering and preparation of the sacrificial animals (D, E).

Directly in front of the offerer was the façade of the Temple. Perhaps the simplest way to gain an idea of its size is to compare it with the Dome of the Rock, and to realize that it presented about twice as much bulk to the viewer, observed from any direction. Twelve steps led up from the court to the threshold of the entrance, which had no doors. The doors were in the next wall dividing the porch (C) from the Holy Place (B), and in front of them in fact (though not in our diagram) stood a feature much admired. It was a golden trellis over which grew a golden vine, and those who wished to make costly gifts to the Temple were encouraged to add gold leaves or grape-clusters. When the doors were standing open a curtain embroidered with a representation of the universe was drawn across the doorway.

Only priests (like Zacharias, Luke I:9) were allowed to enter the Holy Place (B). Twice daily they made the offering of incense there, they tended the seven-branched candlestick, which was lit not with solid candles but with oil lamps, and once a week they set forth fresh showbread on its special table. The walls to the north and south of the Holy Place were hollow, containing passages with small chambers and a staircase leading onto the roof. At the west end of the Holy Place was the veil, a double curtain hiding the innermost sanctuary from view. 'In this,' says Josephus, 'stood nothing whatever. Unapproachable, inviolable, invisible to all, it was called the Holy of Holies' (*War* 5:219).

Of the numerous chambers clustering round the Temple we know little, but the Chamber of Hewn Stone (6) could prove of special interest to us. The Mishnah seems to be telling us that until about the time of Jesus' death the Sanhedrin held its meetings in a chamber of this name, which was close to the Temple itself (*Middoth* 5:5 taken with B. Talmud *A. Zar.* 8b). But we know from Josephus (*War* 5:144)

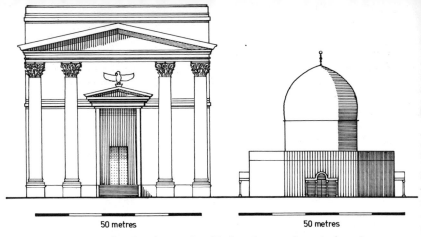

70 Assuming that the cubit mentioned by Josephus was the equivalent of 55 cm (about 21½ in.), the size of the Herodian Temple would compare in this way with the Dome of the Rock

that the *Boulē*, or Council-Chamber, was in or beside a place called the Xystus, which we might translate 'Place of Hewn Stone', and which was evidently just outside the Temple enclosure. It may therefore be that by the time of Jesus' trial the Sanhedrin had just moved its place of meeting outside the Temple enclosure. It may be that it was still inside in the Chamber of Hewn Stone described in the Mishnah. And there is the third possibility that the Mishnah is mistaken, and that the Sanhedrin always met outside the Temple enclosure by the Xystus.

The Sanhedrin, or council, is mentioned first in about 200 BC and gained considerable power under the Hasmoneans. Thus in, or soon after, 47 BC it summoned Herod the Great (then governor of Galilee) to give account to it for his high-handed actions. Besides acting as a court in this way it acted also as an authoritative source of interpretation for the Jewish Law. It also acquired executive power which besides a wide range of lesser powers included also the capacity to impose the death sentence and to declare war. All this took place in its heyday. But already Herod had defied the Sanhedrin when he was called before it as a young man, and when he became King of the Jews ten years later he is said by Josephus to have killed all but one of its members. This body posed a special threat to him because he was not High Priest, as most of his predecessors had been, and therefore not *ex officio* President of the Sanhedrin. In putting its members to death he paved the way for the creation of a Sanhedrin with new membership, but it may well be that the institution never fully recovered its powers as they are described to us in the Mishnah.

After the start of direct Roman rule in A D 6 the Sanhedrin still sat, since without it Jewish religious practice could receive no authoritative direction. On the one hand its powers were formally curtailed, and it was certainly no longer able to execute the death penalty. But on the other hand this council was now the only recognized deliberative body that was distinctly Jewish, and as such it gained in prestige. For a Jew ambitious to become influential among his own people, membership of the Sanhedrin offered the only important avenue to power in the time of Jesus.

Who made up this body with its membership of seventy-one? First there were the 'elders', lay men who were heads of some of the ancient families of the Jewish community, also known as 'the principal men of the people' (Luke XIX:47). Then there were the persons we may picture as a relatively new class of 'graduates'. These were the scribes, who were called by the respectful title 'Rabbi' (My Lord). They were distinguished from other citizens not by their birth or occupation, but by their completion of the prescribed studies. Thus, in contrast with this class, Jesus is described as one who 'has never been taught' (John VII:15). The scribes had first been admitted to the Sanhedrin in about 75 BC, and in Jesus' time most of them belonged to the Pharisees' party.

The third group, which wielded great power, was that of the 'chief priests', mostly of the Sadducean party, whom we may picture as the Chapter of the Temple. The officiating high priest (who seems to have retained the title 'high priest' even when he had laid down his office) was the head, and his closest associates were the captain of the Temple (an adjutant and master of ceremonies), the Temple overseer who held the keys, and the treasurer. This was the innermost group. In fact the directors of the weekly and daily courses of priests technically ranked next to the captain of the Temple. But since these directors came and went they could not, in spite of their status, exercise permanent influence in Jerusalem, and had no right to sit in the Sanhedrin.

As the meeting-place of this central council of Jewry, the Temple symbolized the unity and identity of Jews. We may thus understand how St John's Gospel so often names 'the Jews' as Jesus' opponents in Jerusalem. Obviously Jesus, himself a Jew, did not attack his fellow Jews on racial grounds. Rather he attacked the Jews as Moses attacked the Israelites who 'murmured' against him in the wilderness (Exodus XVII:3, 7; Numbers XXVII:14; compare John VI:41, 52). He was attacking the Jewish establishment, which expressed itself through the decisions of the Sanhedrin, and was visibly present at the heart of Jerusalem in the huge, and doubtless ostentatious, Temple constructed by Herod the Great. Jesus was not, as far as we can see, interested in supporting one of the parties at the expense of the others. But he seems to have seen dangers in the reigning Jewish establishment of his day, as they did in him, and to have made no secret of his views. Hence, as we shall see, his attitude to the Temple, and that of his followers, was ambiguous. While they remained faithful in attending the Temple for teaching and worship they also remained critical of those who controlled it.

The Temple authorities in turn seem, from an early stage in Jesus' public campaign, to have been keeping an eye on his activities. Mark mentions that among the crowds who came to see Jesus were people from Judaea and Jerusalem, and when, in Chapter VII:1–8, some Pharisees and scribes criticize Jesus' disciples for neglecting the laws of purification Jesus retorts that they 'leave the commandment of God and hold fast the tradition of men'. John specifically tells us that Jesus does not trust himself to 'the Jerusalemites' (II:23–5), and Matthew and Luke both give special emphasis to the idea that Jesus' journey to Jerusalem is going to precipitate a crisis (see Matthew XVI:21 and Luke's constant references to the journey in IX:51, XIII:22, 33–35, XVII:11, XIX:11). Mark mentions as those who will have Jesus crucified 'the chief priests and the scribes' and Matthew mentions also 'the elders' (XVI:21), thus indicating the very people who made up the Sanhedrin.

Prophecy at the Presentation
St Luke, alone among the Gospel writers, brings into the early chapters of his Gospel accounts of Jesus being circumcized according to the Law, and, as Mary's first-born son, being presented in the Temple. A child was circumcized wherever the family happened to be on the eighth day after birth, and was on this occasion given a name. Then after thirty-three days when 'the days of her purifying are completed' (Leviticus XII:4), the mother comes to the priest to make a sacrifice and become clean. The prescriptions of Leviticus are in a form which applies to the conditions of the forty years when Moses was leading the Israelites in the wilderness, and says that the woman shall go to the priest 'at the door of the tent of meeting'. But Mary and Joseph went to the Temple, entered the Court of the Gentiles and there bought themselves two pigeons, since the Temple authorities had a

monopoly. Then they passed through the barrier, and climbed up into the Court of the Women. Making towards the foot of the semicircular steps they met Symeon.

Up to this point Mary and Joseph have simply followed what the Law requires. But Luke has already prepared the reader for the uniqueness of Jesus' birth, and Symeon now adds his own prophecy to those of Gabriel (I:26) and Elizabeth (I:41–45). To the theologically inclined reader his words echo Isaiah XL and LII, but – as we have just seen in our description of the Sanhedrin – we should not seek to dissociate theology from political aspirations. Read in a political context Symeon might very well be telling Mary and Joseph that their son was to be a revolutionary leader. Symeon, we are told, was among those 'waiting for the consolation of Israel', a phrase recalling Isaiah XL:1 'Comfort ye, comfort ye, my people.' God prepares salvation, to be the glory of Israel. Jesus will undoubtedly be the downfall of some and the resurgence of others in Israel. And Anna spoke to 'all who were looking for the redemption of Jerusalem' (see Isaiah LII:9).

This language is very close to that of the slogans on coins in the first Jewish War: one of A D 67 saying 'The Freedom of Zion' and one in A D 69, 'For the redemption of Zion'. Again such slogans appear on the coins of the Second War: in A D 132–3, 'Year One of the Redemption of Israel'; or in 133–4, 'For the Freedom of Israel'. Jesus is declared a revolutionary in the very sanctum of the establishment.

When Symeon has told Mary some of the consequences of Jesus' birth they go forward to the steps and up to the gates. There, since the child in their arms shows why they have come, they are soon met by the director of the weekly course of priests. If the Mishnah is correct he takes the two pigeons they have brought, Mary lays her hands on them, and he goes in through the gate, with Joseph perhaps following as far as the step marking the end of the Court of the Israelites. The priest goes to the south-west corner of the Altar and wrings the neck of one of the birds which is a sin-offering. He sprinkles some of its blood on the lower part of the Altar, and allows the rest to run out at a place beside the base of the Altar where there was a drain. Then he puts this bird aside so that he can claim it later on, for the carcase is his. The second bird is a whole-offering, or burnt-offering. This the priest takes to the top of the Altar, mounting by means of the ramp. He goes on a ledge to the south-east corner where he wrings off the bird's head, sprinkles its blood against the upper part of the Altar, and proceeds to gut it. He salts both the head and the body and then throws them on the Altar fire.

The Temple is thus the scene of a ritual with its roots deep in the corporate experience of Israel. Its details, as we learn from the Mishnah, were prescribed minutely. Thus there is said to have been a red line separating the lower part from the upper part of the Altar, and a whole tract in the Mishnah (*Kinnim* by name) explains what to do with bird offerings where one kind of sacrifice can easily be confused with another. How much of this tradition was valuable? Most faithful Jews refused to ask this question because they believed that every detail in the Law was equally valuable and equally God's command. Jesus, however, was to be a revolutionary in that he was ready to question the value even of some commands contained in the Torah – the Law that, for the Jews, forms the most authoritative part of Scripture.

Teaching in the Temple

Luke, characteristically, is the Gospel writer to record a tradition about Jesus coming to the age of maturity. Modern Jews celebrate the ceremony known as the *Bar Mitzvah*, a name meaning 'son of the commandment' in the sense of 'responsible person', for every boy at the age of thirteen, but we know of no comparable ceremony in the Judaism of Jesus' period. At that stage in history, as today, the age of thirteen was the age from which boys were held responsible for their own actions, and were expected to keep the Law in a regular way. The essence of the *Bar Mitzvah* was understood, even though the ceremony we know today was not in its present form; and therefore at the age of thirteen, Jesus, according to Luke II:46, instantly and wonderfully assumes his responsibilities as a student of God's affairs, listening to the teachers in the Temple and asking intelligent questions. We may easily picture him with them in the shade of one of the colonnades.

Combined with the theme of Jesus' intelligence and promise on this occasion we find the theme of Jesus acting independently of his parents. The idea of forsaking father and mother for the sake of sacred studies is common in the later traditions both of Judaism and of Islam. The scholar's detachment and total concentration is symbolized by a jar into which he is to place unread all the letters he receives from his family. He is to keep them in the jar until all his studies are finished, and only then may he read them. It may well be that the account of Jesus as a boy spending time with the teachers in the Temple is a genuine childhood memory preserved by the members of Jesus' family. But as things turned out, the destiny he was to fulfil was very different from that of a learned scribe.

The Temptation at the Pinnacle

The second of Jesus' temptations appears, if we are to judge by his response to it, to be an attempt to force God into an answer. It is recorded by both Matthew and Luke, though there is no material difference between them (see Matthew IV, and Luke IV). The devil takes Jesus to Jerusalem (according to Luke), i.e., 'The Holy City' (Matthew), and sets him on some lofty point known as the 'pinnacle' ('little wing') of the Temple. This may possibly have been one of the side-pieces of the façade, containing the rooms marked 7 and 8 on Ill. 68. It is mentioned, perhaps, because the Temple roof was an obvious high point, but also because the Temple provided a context in which belief in God's word would be heightened. The devil quotes a Psalm, and Jesus replies very much in rabbinic style by citing the Scriptures Deuteronomy VI: 16 'Thou shalt not tempt the Lord thy God.'

After Titus' destruction nothing much remained of the Temple proper, but a good deal of the stonework in the lower courses of the enclosure wall was never dismantled. The stones of the south-east corner of the Temple area (compare Ills. 71 and 72) were the least disturbed. Herodian stones can be seen to this day reaching almost to the top of the corner, and from Titus' destruction until the Umayyad reconstruction, which is to say for the whole late Roman and Byzantine period, the masonry at this corner stood like the ruin of a great tower, forming the most obvious high point of its period and the only one of its size at the site of Herod's Temple. Of all the ruins which remained it seemed the most natural setting for the story of the temptation and was understood to be so by local Christians. But it has – unfortunately – no claim to this identification.

Jesus' Pilgrimages to the Feasts

Mark, Matthew, and Luke present their Gospels in two parts, the first dealing with Jesus' Galilean campaign and the second with the final conflict in Jerusalem. The Gospel according to St John is arranged differently, since it mentions several occasions on which Jesus comes from Galilee to Jerusalem before his final journey. Jesus is portrayed as coming to the city, like most Jews of his time, as a pilgrim to one of the festivals. He is, so to speak, a foreigner in Jerusalem, coming only for feasts.

John tells of three feasts: two of these are the spring feast of the Passover, which provided both the occasion for the cleansing of the Temple (John II: 13) and the setting for the culmination of Jesus' life; and the autumn feast of Tabernacles (John VII: 2), 'which is

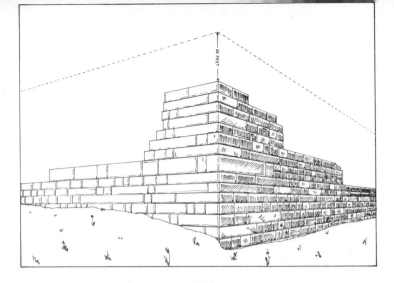

20 FEET

71 The Herodian stones at the south-east corner as they may have looked immediately after the Temple's destruction by Titus in AD 70. Later on, this corner, being the loftiest of the surviving remains, was identified by Christians with the 'Pinnacle of the Temple'

72 At the south-east corner of the Temple enclosure the large stones of Herod's architects rise almost to the top of the present walls

considered especially sacred and important by the Hebrews' (Josephus, *Antiquities* 8 : 100), and at which the daily whole-offering in the Temple was followed by a special libation of water brought from Siloam. It is possible that the occasion of the healing at the pool near the Sheep Gate was also the feast of Tabernacles, since this was sometimes simply called 'the Feast', which is the name given it in John V : 1 in several manuscripts (though the best simply say 'a feast'), and the passage about the woman taken in adultery was placed in this context. The third feast mentioned is Dedication, or Hanukkah (John X : 22), a December feast celebrating the re-dedication of the Temple after it had been profaned in 165 BC by Antiochus Epiphanes. This feast was and still is specially celebrated by the lighting of lamps.

Jesus, according to John VII : 14, 'went up into the Temple and taught', thus assuming the rights of a scribe. When he first teaches, his authority is questioned and 'the Jews', as opposed to the ordinary people listening to his teaching, begin to suspect he might be the Messiah. 'The chief priests and the Pharisees', or probably the available members of the Sanhedrin, sent the Temple police, Levites who were specially appointed, to arrest him (VII : 32), but they could not bring themselves to do so (VII : 45). A similar clash with the Sanhedrin is associated by Mark with Jesus' final visit to Jerusalem (Mark XI : 27–33). At this point Matthew adds the damaging story of the two sons, one of whom said he would go and work in his father's vineyard and did not, while the other refused, but then changed his mind and went (Matthew XXI : 28–32). After another equally embarrassing story (Mark XII : 1–11) the 'chief priests and scribes and elders' (Mark XI : 27) tried to arrest him, but 'feared the multitude'. Mark gives further examples of Jesus' rabbinic style of teaching in the Temple (XII : 13–37) and an additional condemnation of the scribes (XII : 38–40) and ends the teaching in the Temple with the story of the Widow's Mite (XII : 41–44). This offering was made into a box that tapered like a trumpet, the regular shape everywhere for almsboxes both in the provinces and in the Temple. Of the thirteen in the Court of the Women six were labelled 'Free-Will Offerings'.

Jesus' attitude to the Temple is partly expressed in the symbolic action of driving out the traders, a demonstration that we consider later on. But the ambiguity of his approach seems to be summed up in his final Jerusalem routine. On the one hand, Luke tells us, he spent those last days in Jerusalem teaching in the Temple, attracting everyone to come and hear him (XXI : 38). On the other hand, as he comes out of the Temple (Mark XIII : 1), one of the disciples says

'Look, Teacher, what wonderful stones and what wonderful buildings' and Jesus replies: 'Do you see these great buildings? There will not be left here one stone upon another that will not be thrown down.' While the Temple stood it seems that Jesus (unlike the Qumran community) suggested no substitute. But he refused to treat the great building, its institutions, and the members of its establishment as though they would stand for ever.

Five Demonstrations

Of the miracles and symbolic acts done by Jesus in Jerusalem five served as public demonstrations, or at least were so interpreted by the authorities. Were it not for John's Gospel we should know few of them, but John takes a special interest in what took place in Jerusalem. Postponing study of the cleansing of the Temple until the place assigned it by Mark in his presentation of Jesus' ministry, we begin with the healing at Bethesda.

At Bethesda

The Copper Scroll found at Qumran was written in Aramaic, probably in about AD 100. It gives a list of places where treasure is found, and the largest concentration was hidden in four places at a pool of 'Beth-esdatain'. The writing is not entirely legible and the letters 'd' and 't' could be 'r' and 'h', producing 'Bethesrahain'. But the first version is the most likely because it seems to fit with a place named in different manuscripts of John's Gospel 'Bethesda', 'Bethzatha', or 'Bethsaida'. Since 'Beth-esdatain' seemingly means 'Two Bethesdas', the manuscripts of John that write 'Bethesda' therefore seem to be following the Semitic form of the name. But in its Greek form the name became slightly changed, since the 'sd' is altered to 'z', and the consonants 'th' and 'z' were then exchanged. So Josephus, writing in Greek at about the same time as the making of the Copper Scroll, writes 'the Bezetha'. The form 'Bethzatha' looks like a mistaken attempt to alter the nonsense form of the Greek into something with a meaning – a very frequent habit of the scribes – for 'Beth-zatha' means 'House of Oil', and 'Beth-saida', meaning 'House of Nobility', may be another attempt inspired by the same motive.

The meaning of the name Bethesda, assuming this is to be the original form, could be 'House of Mercy' (*beth chesedah*), and it was used, according to Josephus, to mean the rising ground to the north of the Temple area or the housing district that we have suggested was built on it in the time of Herod the Great. This housing district was also known as the Kainopolis, or 'New City'.

Why was the area named Bethesda? Let us speculate that it was because of a 'House of Mercy', which was the principal building in the area. As we have argued when making the city plan, Herod the Great deliberately created a street which would lead across two pools to something on their east side. Did it lead to the 'House of Mercy'?

The Copper Scroll says in sections 57 and 58 (3Q 15 xi 12), 'Near there at Bethesdatain: in the pool, where one goes into the small pool is a jar of aloe wood and one of resin of white pine. Near there at the west entry of the porch of the Triclinium near the place for the Stove is nine hundred talents of silver and five talents of gold.' Two other hiding-places are also mentioned at Bethesdatain. If this passage is correctly translated it shows that there was indeed a building as well as a pool at Bethesda.

Here we need to look back for a moment at the directions given in John's Gospel, Chapter V. The New English Bible translates verse 2 as follows: 'Now at the Sheep-pool in Jerusalem there is a place with five colonnades. Its name in the language of the Jews is Bethesda.' We might paraphrase this translation in the light of what we have studied to read 'Now at the Sheep-pool in Jerusalem is "the Bethesda" (as it is called in Hebrew) with five colonnades.'

We may also look on to later usage, for the pool is almost always in later Christian tradition called 'the Sheep-pool', and the name Bethesda (or its variants) seems to drop out of use.

The scene of the healing we are about to study is therefore not necessarily a pool, but (as witnessed by two later pilgrims, one of about the eighth century and the other of the twelfth century) perhaps a building with five porticoes or porches which was beside a pool. This was the Sheep-pool, but it was also the pool associated with (or 'of') Bethesda, as we see in the Copper Scroll.

Let us look more closely at the terrain. Ills. 73 and 74 show the positions of the main landmarks. There is a pool, now half filled in outside the city wall near St Stephen's Gate. It is called The Pool of the Bath of Our Lady Mary, a bath-house in the building adjoining the tree inside the gate. On the left inside the gate, until it was recently levelled to make the market area and car park that appear in the air photo, the large Pool of Israel ran along the north wall of the Haram esh Sharif, which is probably the line of the northern portico of Herod's Court of the Gentiles. Farther along the wall are the lofty buildings of the Umariya School, which replace the Antonia fortress of Jesus' day. To

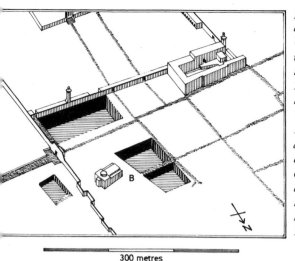

73 *A diagram of the area shown below. The Umariya School (top right) occupies the site of the Antonia castle. Below the minaret on the left is the Pool of Israel. To the right of St Anne's are the two pools at Bethesda (also known as the Sheep-pool) and outside the wall is another pool belonging to the same system and now known as The Pool of the Bath of our Lady Mary*

B

300 metres

74 *The north end of the Haram esh Sharif and the adjoining area Bethesda seen from the north-east, showing St Anne's Church (arrow)*

the north of the Pool of Israel is St Anne's Church, whose alignment depends on its original association with the twin pools to its west. These formed the Sheep-pool. But, as the air photograph shows, the pool was filled in, and a large yard containing some trees is now there to the west of the church. A deep trench has been dug at the north end of the larger pool next to the causeway, the east end of which has been strengthened by the addition of a row of five modern buttresses. Nothing, however, is visible now above ground of the smaller pool. Beside the church and to its north, near the letter B on the diagram (Ill. 73), the photograph shows an excavated area.

The shape of the Pool of Israel and the Sheep-pool was adapted to a valley. The pools were partly cut into the rock, but the valley reduced the amount of cutting required, and their level was controlled by dams across the valley. The arrangement can be seen in Ills. 75 and 76, which show the north-west corner of the large pool, with cutting into the rock on the bottom, and a masonry wall built on top of the rock where it was necessary to complete the dam or causeway separating the two pools, and carry the street across them. Ill. 77 shows the complexity of the remains in area B, looking north from a point near St Anne's Church. To the right of the remains of the column at the far side of the trench is a low wide hole in the rock. Inside it is the small plastered cave shown in Ill. 78. It is nearly 2 metres (6 feet) square, and has at the bottom what might be described as a basin or sump. It is entered by steps (from which the photograph was taken). Elsewhere in area B there are signs of other similar caves, similarly arranged. All were in use in Jesus' day.

Are we looking at the remains of the 'House of Mercy'? Since point B forms the destination of the street this seems a reasonable assumption, though the remains so far discovered are scrappy and hard to interpret. An attempt has been made to show that the cave was arranged, as in an Aesculapian healing sanctuary, to enable a sick person to sleep, and, when he had received the appropriate dream, to wash and be healed. But the bottom of the little cave is too small for anyone to lie down, and the whole arrangement is strongly reminiscent of a cistern. The little cave is therefore not likely to give us much idea of the use of the building to which it belonged.

75 (opposite above) The north-west corner of the large south pool at Bethesda showing how it was cut into living rock (lower arrow). The buttresses at the end of the excavation are a modern addition, but the masonry and plaster (upper arrow) on the right side of the pool are ancient

76 (opposite below) At the north-east corner of the same pool the living rock (arrow) came nearer to the surface than at the north-west corner

77 In the excavations at area B, Ill. 73, the remains of Jesus' time have
been overbuilt by both a pagan sanctuary of the period after AD 135 and a

Byzantine church. To the right of the large column base in the foreground is the opening of a small cave (arrow)

78 Inside a plastered cave (Ill. 77) with a basin, or sump, in the bottom, in the excavation at Bethesda. Several similar caves seem to have existed in the area of the excavation, and were in use in the time of Jesus

The later history of the site, however, provides strong support for John's Gospel in its assertion that it was a place of healing, and that in its five porches were lying a crowd of sick people. We know from the many small offerings found near site B that the place was used as a healing sanctuary (possibly a Serapeum) from AD 135, when the Roman official cults were installed in the city. We also know that by the middle of the fifth century AD the Christians had built their first church there, which covered over and effectively sealed off the previous buildings at site B. This is the church to which the Byzantine columns belonged. Probably this site of the church was deliberately chosen in order to suppress the pagan cult, since we know of other pagan sites deliberately obliterated by Christian buildings, e.g. at Bethlehem, or the Holy Sepulchre in Jerusalem.

In Antiquity a great deal of faith was placed in healing sanctuaries, and people of many different religious faiths were anxious to seek benefit from them. We find for instance that the healing baths near Tiberias and Gadara continued in use as healing places from Jewish times through to Christian, and that in Christian times the sick persons slept in the sanctuary, awaited a dream, washed, and were healed in just the same sequence followed in pagan Aesculapia. Hence there is some likelihood that in using the site as a healing sanctuary after AD 135 the Romans were simply continuing a tradition already established in or before the time of Herod the Great. If so, the sanctuary as Jesus had known it would almost certainly have been under the supervision of Jews, but they must almost certainly have been regarded as gravely unorthodox. Indeed the immediate reaction of 'the Jews' is to question the orthodoxy of the man who has been cured by Jesus. Cyril of Jerusalem, preaching about Bethesda just before AD 348, speaks of 'a great infidelity of the Jews' there. At any rate it is unlikely that the sanctuary was already in pagan hands by the time of Jesus, since John could hardly have failed to mention the fact in his Gospel, and it is in any case extremely unlikely that any pagan establishment could have flourished so close to the Temple.

Jesus' demonstration took place in a building that archaeological examination suggests may already have been destroyed and replaced by another in AD 135. What the five porches were like or where they were can therefore be known only by further archaeological work – if indeed anything of them has survived. This means that Christians visiting the site later had to explain things as best they could. Thus Origen in his Commentary on St John's Gospel explains that the five porches surrounded not the sanctuary building but the pools, 'four round the edges and one across the middle'. The healing was then thought to have taken place at the pool – after all was there not a 'troubling of water'? It is improbable, however, that sick people could hurry to throw themselves into pools as deep and inaccessible as those

79 At the north-east corner the rock was excavated to a depth of nearly 15 metres (50 feet). This view from the north-west shows how the pool was filled with earth, visible with its diagonal strata (arrow) in the right-hand wall. This seems to have been done during the period of the Latin kingdom

of the Sheep-pool, but much more likely that they did so somewhere on site B with its multitude of smaller water installations.

The healing of the paralyzed man has a beneficial effect on the humane level. Jesus intervenes of his own accord so that the man, with his sickness and inhibitions, is set free from what paralyzed him. The healing is also a sign, pointing to the aim of Jesus' mission 'that they might have life and have it abundantly' (John X: 10). The man can be taken to represent a stagnating and paralyzed official establishment, lost in matters of secondary importance. Hence the threat presented by a reformer like Jesus, and hence the sharpness of both the official reaction and the crisis that Jesus now provokes.

At Siloam

A second demonstration provokes a new crisis – this time for a person who expresses loyalty to Jesus. Jesus heals a man blind from birth (John IX: 1). There is no hint that the man asked for healing, and the place where Jesus and his disciples found him is not specified. The disciples ask Jesus just the sort of question which students would address to a scribe, which involves the highly technical notion of a person being able to sin before birth. They even address him as 'Rabbi'. Jesus responds by denying the disciples' suggestion, and then says three things, which provide meanings for the action he then takes in curing the man's blindness. First, that what is now to be done for the man is a work of God; second, that the time available for such works is limited; and, finally, that it is Jesus' mission to be a light in the world.

The last Jerusalem demonstration we examined, involving contact between Jesus and a healing sanctuary, appeared to have been glaringly unorthodox. In this demonstration Jesus, himself, uses a procedure that was unorthodox, at least in the sense that it was not prescribed in Jewish tradition. Indeed, C. K. Barrett, in his classic commentary on John's Gospel, quotes an inscription describing a rather similar procedure inspired by a pagan god: 'To Valerius Aper, a blind soldier, the god revealed that he should go and take the blood of a white cock with honey and rub them into an eyesalve and anoint his eyes three days. And he received his sight, and came and gave thanks publicly to the god.' (H. Deissmann, *Inscriptiones Latinae Selectae*, 132). But from an unorthodox start, making clay with spittle and anointing the man's eyes, Jesus goes on to do something firmly within the scope of Jewish practice, even though not exactly commanded. As Naaman the Syrian was sent away to wash in the Jordan so this man is now sent to wash in Siloam. Jews had used Siloam as a source of water for purification both in the elaborate ceremonial of the Red Heifer, so we are told in the Mishnah (*Parah* 3:2), and for the water poured out before the Lord at the feast of Tabernacles (*Sukkah* 4:9). Probably they went to Siloam because for them it represented the spring of David's Jerusalem. Indeed, Josephus regularly calls Siloam a 'spring'.

As a matter of fact Siloam was not exactly this. In the early days when David captured the city it had depended for its water on the spring at Gihon. But as the city began to grow the arrangements at this spring became increasingly inconvenient, and a channel was cut along the hillside just above the road shown running along the Kidron Valley (see Ill. 81). The water from Gihon was collected in a pool constructed for the purpose, the lower pool at Siloam, which is now used as a garden. The name of this system, 'the Shiloah' means 'the sender'.

This pool and tunnel were both vulnerable to military attack. When Hezekiah was preparing for an invasion by the Assyrians at the end of the eighth century BC he therefore improved the defences by cutting a new channel underground, marked by the dotted line, and (probably) by excavating a new receiving pool a little higher up the Tyropoeon Valley. It seems probable that at this point the line of the city wall corresponded roughly with the road that runs along the two northern edges of the lower pool, which is the best available line for defence, and that the upper pool was made in order to provide a collection-point inside the new line of wall.

The upper pool at Siloam is shown in Ill. 80. What now appears is a long pool coming out from an arch underneath a mosque. It is still fed by Hezekiah's underground channel, which comes in from behind it: Ill. 80 shows the narrow shape of the present pool and the channel as they relate to the remains of the pool at an earlier period. These remains were first explored by Dr H. Guthe on behalf of the German Palestine Society in 1880, and then in 1896 for the British Palestine Exploration Fund by the archaeologist F. J. Bliss and the architect A. C. Dickie. Their findings did not determine the date of the arrangements they describe, and we cannot be sure if they were dealing with Herodian remains (in which case Jesus would have been familiar with them) or with a later adaptation by Hadrian, who is known to have built somewhere in Jerusalem a Shrine of the Four Nymphs.

The visitor to this pool in the Herodian or Roman period made his approach by descending a stepped street in the Tyropoeon Valley. The street runs along the side of the pool and, as it does so, descends steeply, going down 8 metres (26 feet) in a horizontal distance of about

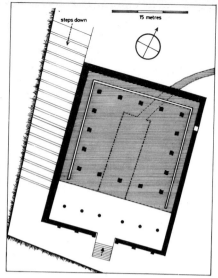

80 The upper Pool of Siloam: the remains discovered include a low wall standing in the water just inside the main perimeter wall. The dotted lines show the extent of the modern pool and the direction from which it is fed by Hezekiah's tunnel

25 metres (82 feet), a gradient of one in three. Turning left at the bottom the visitor walked along the south-east wall of the pool to a door that admitted him to the covered gallery giving access to the edge of the water. In the water stood sixteen pillars supporting the roof arches, and on these rested a wooden roof covered with tiles, open in the middle to the sky. Round the pool was a low wall 75 centimetres (2½ feet) high, whose function is not immediately obvious. If it were simply a seat it ought to have openings to allow users of the pool to walk through. More probably it once divided the dirtier water (into which people would first step) from the cleaner water in the central section. Very little can be seen today of these masonry remains. Several column drums stand in the water of the pool, and there is a short section of ancient moulding immediately east of the mosque.

We thus have a fairly detailed knowledge of the upper pool, which Christians since before AD 333 have treated as the Pool of Siloam mentioned in John, Chapter IX. But Josephus, whenever he gives any indication of the whereabouts of the 'Spring of Siloam', says that it was outside the city wall, and this certainly had been the position of the original pool of the Shiloah system. If therefore we heed Josephus, this lower pool, now called Birket el Hamra, must have been the 'Pool of Siloam' mentioned in John's Gospel.

Why did Christians in later times transfer the name to the upper pool? If it had indeed been Hadrian's sanctuary of the Nymphs, Christians may have wished to substitute a commemoration of their

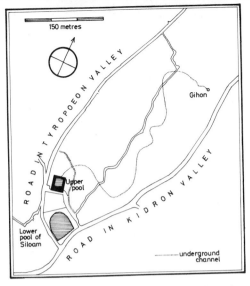

81 The two Pools of Siloam lie at the intersection of the roads coming down the Tyropoeon and the Kidron Valleys. The spring at Gihon, which is the source of the water reaching the pools, was probably hidden underground in the time of Jesus, and few if any of the citizens of Jerusalem in that period realized that the underground channel that fed the pools was artificial, or knew its origin

82 The area of the Pool of Siloam seen from the east. The road running down the Tyropoeon Valley is on the left, and the upper end of the lower pool site (arrow) is marked by the fig trees at the bottom left

own. The name is therefore likely to have been transferred very soon after Constantine's rise to power, and the ascendancy of the Christian community in Jerusalem, say between AD 315 and 325.

The man whom Jesus cured by sending him to Siloam was not left alone for long. First some Pharisees interrogated him unofficially, and then 'the Jews' took over and held an official examination. As a result the man was excommunicated.

The Raising of Lazarus

When Jesus was told that his friend Lazarus was sick he delayed setting out to help him for two days, according to John XI:6. By any ordinary reckoning such a delay was heartless, since it caused suffering to Lazarus' sisters Mary and Martha that could have been avoided. But Jesus, as presented in John's account, is not trying to do the humane thing. He has an overriding motive, which makes his delay deliberate. Not only does Jesus not apologize for it, he says 'For your sake I am glad that I was not there, so that you may believe' (John XI:15). For this demonstration is surely designed to make the point that Jesus'

83 The ancient moulding (arrow) in the masonry of the north wall of the upper Pool of Siloam. More exists but is now covered up. While the moulding might have been made in the Roman period, the column base in the picture was probably made for the Byzantine church that overhung the pool

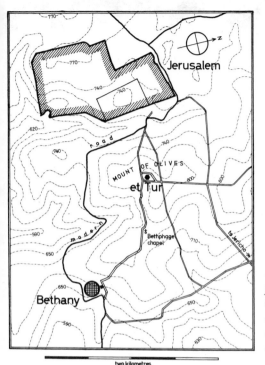

84 *Jerusalem's eastern approaches. The road from Jericho in Jesus' day came in on the right of the diagram, but today's main road approaches through Bethany*

power is enough to defy and overmaster death. In this perspective we may understand R. H. Lightfoot's judgment that the raising of Lazarus was 'the Lord's crowning act of His ministry'.

Jesus sets out for Bethany from Peraea, Herod Antipas' territory on the east of the River Jordan, crosses the Jordan, and goes to Jericho. From the site of that city, so far below sea level, he climbs to Jerusalem by the main road. Doubtless the road of his time followed much the same line as the Roman road, which was paved a century or two later, and the line of the paved road can be seen to this day along most of its length. As this road nears the Mount of Olives there is a crossroads: the quickest way to Jerusalem is straight ahead, where the road ascends steeply up to the lowest point on the Mount of Olives and from that makes its way down into the Kidron Valley for its final short climb to the city walls. The track to the left leads to Bethany, so Martha and Mary would have come to meet Jesus on this track before they took him to the tomb.

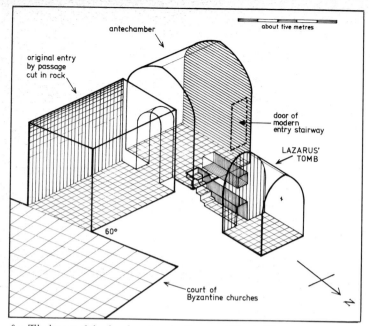

85 The layout of the chambers forming Lazarus' Tomb. The original entry was by the passage on the left, which ends in the present mosque and has been blocked. The present entry is by a staircase pierced through the rock in the seventeenth century and coming in by the north wall of the antechamber. In the floor of the antechamber is an opening with steps leading into the tunnel to the tomb chamber

86 (opposite above) El Aizariya, the village which occupies the site of biblical Bethany, from the north, with the religious buildings in the foreground. The Franciscans' Church of the Raising of Lazarus is on the left, there is a mosque with a sunken courtyard in the middle, and a new Greek Orthodox church is on the right. A few metres down the track to the left of the Greek church is a notice (arrow) on the wall, directly above the present entrance to the Tomb of Lazarus

Not many buildings of ancient Bethany have ever been excavated, but a great deal of pottery from the New Testament period has been found scattered on the surface of the soil in the area marked on Ill. 84 by a circle. We therefore know pretty well where the village was, and we know too the archaeological development of the religious buildings that grew up near what is now called the Tomb of Lazarus. Apart from the religious buildings the village of Bethany seems to have been abandoned in about the fourteenth century A D. But if it was in the area suggested by the pottery then it would be reasonable to

88 (above) Some of the masonry in the west wall of Lazarus' Tomb has been removed and reveals the living rock, behind the metre stick. But there is no sign of a tomb shelf

87 (left) Looking down the manhole into the passage leading from the antechamber to Lazarus' Tomb. Only masonry is visible, and no rock

describe it as fifteen furlongs from the Temple, counting a furlong (or stade) as 183 metres (600 feet). This assumes that the journey along the track went through the village on the Mount of Olives called et Tur, since the journey along the modern main road is about half as long again.

The modern visitor is shown a 'Tomb of Lazarus' cut deep into rock. The limestone has rotted, and it is no longer possible to be sure what shape it was originally, but at the moment it comprises two rooms. The surfaces visible, however, are all masonry or plaster, except in the west wall of the supposed tomb chamber (marked by a cross in Ill. 85), where the masonry has been broken and some decaying rock can be seen through the hole.

Present-day visitors have to reach the tomb by a staircase made by the Franciscans soon after 1610. It enters the antechamber through a hole in the north wall, and in the interest of simplicity only the position of the hole has been shown in our diagram. The original entry had been by the passage on the left (the east), now blocked up. The tomb chamber to the north of the antechamber must at present be approached by a manhole in the floor of the antechamber and a low passage through which the visitor has to crawl. Above the passage is a window, and our diagram has been simplified by showing both the window and the passage as longer than they really are.

The building at the near (east) end of the original entry passage, now a mosque, was built in the ruins of a Christian church first developed in the fourth century. But the mosque and the churches that preceded it were all on the same alignment, and it is therefore of special interest that the passage meets the mosque at an angle of sixty degrees and not at right angles. This suggests that both the tomb chambers and the passage existed before the first church, and thus that the church was built at a site which was already venerated as Lazarus' Tomb. Could it be the very tomb mentioned in John's Gospel? It is very likely that it was a tomb (even though no positive archaeological evidence can be seen to support the tradition) and it seems certain that it is in the area of the New Testament village of Bethany. So possibly it is authentic.

But if it were authentic it could in its present condition shed very little light on the Gospel narrative. It has been suggested that the manhole in the floor of the antechamber is original, and that this would fit the words that a stone lay 'upon' it, as we read in the Latin and English versions of the Bible, in John XI: 38–39. But both these translations render a Greek word which could equally well mean 'against', and there is nothing in the wording of the Gospel to tell us whether the stone that was removed was lying vertically or horizontally. Again the insignificant amount of rock now visible in the tomb does not enable us to work out the original floor levels (as shown by Ill. 87). But we may guess that the present awkward arrangement has come about largely because the level of the floor, at least in the antechamber, has risen through falls of rotten limestone from the ceiling. This is a common development in such caves, and if it took place in ours the floor levels of the antechamber and tomb chamber might originally have been the same.

Though the tomb itself provides us with little or no useful information to help us in understanding the Gospel, we should not forget that as a demonstration the raising of Lazarus has the effect of raising the temperature of the conflict between Jesus and the establishment. As soon as the Pharisees receive news of what Jesus has done they and the chief priests call a meeting of the Sanhedrin. They try to re-formulate their policy in face of Jesus' growing popularity. Thus Caiaphas the high priest, speaking more wisely than he knew (see John XI: 49–52), reiterated the official decision that Jesus has to die. This is not, of course, a new policy (for earlier expressions of it see John VII: 1 and 25, VIII: 37 and 40), but it is now presented as a formal policy of the highest Jewish authority of the day.

King on a Donkey

The average Christian today sees the Bible partly through his use of it in church services. Thus such a person will have a vivid picture of Jesus' triumphal entry into Jerusalem on Palm Sunday, which gets its name because of the palms the children were carrying when they welcomed Jesus. It is perhaps useful to remember that Mark, whose account of the triumphal entry probably forms the basis for all the rest, says nothing about Sunday, nor about children, nor about palms, though of course he does speak about garments and branches (Mark XI: 8). John's is the Gospel which mentions palms (XII: 13).

Mark's account, which is followed by Matthew and Luke, presents the triumphal entry as the demonstration that marks the final and most significant stage in Jesus' journey up to Jerusalem from Galilee and, more immediately, from Jericho. According to these three Gospels we ought therefore to picture Jesus coming on the main Jericho-Jerusalem road to the same crossroads we discussed in the last section, shown at the right of Ill. 84. Thus, in the words of Mark XI: 1, he is drawing near 'to Jerusalem, to Bethphage and Bethany, at the Mount of Olives', and this is a realistic way of describing the point he has reached if we accept the identification of Bethphage with et Tur on the summit of the Mount of Olives. Luke reproduces Mark's wording here, but Matthew makes a slight change. For him Jesus comes right into Bethphage (XXI: 1) before he sends the disciples into 'the village facing us'. This expression is hard to interpret, since what faces et Tur village (assuming it to have been Bethphage) is the city of Jerusalem.

In several instances we find that later Jerusalem pilgrimage guides and the Jerusalem liturgy relied far more on the Gospel of Matthew than on that of Mark. Hence we may suppose that they began to look for a site for Bethphage that fitted Matthew's phrasing. Early in the fifth century it had been identified with a place where there was a chapel formerly believed to be 'where Lazarus' sister Mary met the Lord'. This is the site now occupied by the modern Bethphage chapel belonging to the Franciscans, shown on Ill. 84. We have not very much evidence for this transfer of Bethphage from its position at et Tur to the place with the chapel, but we can be sure that if we are right in thinking of Bethphage as having been 'on the Mount of Olives' (as Eusebius says) in the sense that it was on the very summit, like modern et Tur, then the memory of Bethphage would have been over-shadowed quite early in the fourth century by the building of Constantine's Eleona church there. It would consequently have been reasonable to move the place where Bethphage was remembered, and in any case the move may perhaps have been only to the other end of the same village.

Ill. 89 shows part of the road from Bethany to Jerusalem, with the modern Bethphage chapel indistinctly visible just beyond the trees in the foreground. The road goes on to et Tur (in sunlight with the large Carmelite convent on its left) and from there descends out of sight on the far side of the Mount of Olives. A path can just be seen ascending towards St Stephen's Gate in the city wall. So if we wish to picture the route of Jesus on his triumphal entry we shall, if we follow Mark's account, think of him mounting the colt somewhere between the crossroads on the Jericho-Jerusalem road and et Tur (or even Bethany). If we follow Matthew this imprecision is reduced, and we know that he mounted the ass and began the procession at Bethphage. Then our only point of doubt is whether Bethphage was at et Tur.

Evidently Jesus had made prior arrangements for the arrival. What was he hoping to achieve by this demonstration? Perhaps it is to show the crowd (which is somehow present) that he is a king, perhaps not. But it is quite clear that the crowd treats him as king, for they spread

89 The road from Bethany to Jerusalem. Bethany is out of sight below the bottom of the picture, and the modern Bethphage chapel is just beyond the trees at the bottom. The road leads on to et Tur, the village at the top of the wooded area, and then disappears down the far side of the Mount of Olives before climbing up to the city walls

their garments in front of him, as the Israelites had for Jehu of old when he had just been anointed king (see II Kings IX:13). This gesture and their shouts of welcome combine to make their meaning clear, and the throwing of branches could hardly be intended to evoke the wave-offering of the *lulab* (four branches) at the feast of Tabernacles, since the branches at the triumphal entry were not waved but thrown on the ground, and the entry is explicitly placed in the context of Passover (in April) and not that of Tabernacles (in October).

The words of the people welcoming Jesus have strong political force. They comprise words from a psalm:

Hosanna (meaning, 'Save now!'). Blessed is he who comes in the name of the Lord! (Psalm CXVIII:25–26).

And an extempore addition, perhaps a slogan prepared for the occasion:

Blessed is the coming kingdom of our father David!
Hosanna in the highest!

It sounds as though the political hints that were heard at Jesus' presentation in the Temple are now beginning to be fulfilled. In Luke's version the political threat of the demonstration is increased not only by his added words that the people were a 'crowd of disciples' (XIX:37 – are these the 'brotherhood of 120' of Acts I:15 ?), but also by his variation on Psalm CXVIII:26, 'Blessed is *the king* who comes in the name of the Lord!'

Matthew makes the same point in a different and ingenious way by identifying the colt with the one mentioned in Zechariah IX:9, the prophecy which reads 'Behold, thy king cometh unto thee, meek and sitting upon an ass, upon a colt the foal of a beast of burden', nor is the point weakened by Matthew's added note that the crowd identifies Jesus as 'the prophet from Nazareth' (XXI:11). Matthew's, after all, is the Gospel in which the Magi ask Herod, 'Where is he that is born King of the Jews?'

All the Gospels present the idea of Jesus' trial, and in all of them Pilate asks whether he says he is King of the Jews (see Mark XV:2). If, as we have seen, the triumphal entry was a pre-arranged demonstration and Jesus intended it to express his kingship, then we have to see it in the context of his own forebodings if we are to grasp the special way in which he takes his power. Jesus, as he receives the welcome of the crowd at the triumphal entry, knows that he is entering the city where he has to face his most powerful and bitter opponents, and that he is likely to die. The difficulty of understanding kingship in these terms is illustrated by the mere handful of followers who seem to have persevered in following him when it came to the moment of his crucifixion.

Cleansing for the Temple

In John's Gospel the climax to Jesus' demonstrations was the raising of Lazarus, in the sense that it was a display of victory over the last enemy, death. But in the structure of Mark and the other two Gospel writers the climax seems to come at the moment when Jesus penetrates the Temple and 'cleanses' it (Mark XI:11, 15). The immediate moral to be drawn from his action is that a place that should be consecrated to prayer is instead (as Jeremiah had once said, in Jeremiah VII:11) turned into 'a den of robbers'. But this criticism is not levelled at dishonest traders in the Temple. Dishonesty was not, to be sure, unknown; but if this had been Jesus' meaning he would hardly at the same time have prevented people from carrying loads through the Temple (Mark XI:16), for this is a regulation concerning reverence, not honesty. The Mishnah has a telling, though not exact, parallel when it forbids those who enter the Temple to wear their travelling (working?) clothes and says 'A man may not enter the Temple with his staff or his sandal or his wallet, or with the dust upon his feet; nor may he make a short cut of it' (*Berakhoth* 9:5, see also Luke IX:3). Rather, Jesus was reminding those who used the Temple area that its primary purpose was for prayer. Trade then, even honest trade, is not its purpose, and in this demonstration Jesus perhaps intended to call into question the immense financial and economic power of the Temple and, in consequence, the standing of official Judaism as an institution. He contrasts the essential and the accidental, the permanent and the transitory. And Matthew here implies, by his account of the crowds who flock to Jesus in the Temple, a contrast between the effectiveness of Jesus and the ineffectiveness of the Temple authorities.

We do not know precisely where the shops and money-changers did their business in the Temple. Shops were there because the Temple authorities exercised a monopoly over the sale of sacrificial animals, and there had to be money-changers to enable persons offering money to make their offering in the correct coinage. Tyrian coinage was the standard for most payments: the silver coin with the head of the pagan

Melkart on it as we have seen in Ill. 31 (*Bekhoroth* 8:7). The time for paying shekel dues came in March, and three weeks before payment was due a warning was supposed to be given (as prescribed in Mishnah *Shekalim* 1:1, 3). 'On the twenty-fifth of Adar the tables were set up in the Temple', but these are hardly likely to be the tables of the money-changers. Rather the Mishnah is here speaking of the tables of those who were receiving the payment, which would already have to be in an acceptable currency. Money-changers – extra busy at the time of these payments – would in fact have been needed in the Temple all the year round.

By cleansing the Temple Jesus demonstrates that the Temple is being wrongly used, and requires improvement, but he is not rejecting Temple worship out of hand. For the time being (for he is presented as telling the disciples that its days are numbered) the Temple is to be accepted as the place of worship *par excellence*. He himself continues to go there and so, after his death, do his disciples, hard though that discipline sometimes proved.

The Inner Meaning

Not long before his crucifixion, perhaps on the Tuesday or the Wednesday of the same week, Jesus went as usual to Bethany and there, according to Mark XIV: 3–9, he was sitting as a guest at supper when a woman came up to him with a vessel in her hand containing expensive salve. Breaking the vessel, she anointed his head, once again recalling Jehu (see II Kings IX:6). Jesus' demonstrations seem to have made their mark, for he is treated as some kind of king, and will be identified as such by the label on his cross (Mark XV: 26). But his is not to be a painless triumph. The anointing which befits a king is also, as Jesus tells those at table with him, an anointing of his body for burial (Mark XIV: 8). Personally, Jesus shows that he is aware that threats against him have now gathered so much momentum that a crisis cannot be far off. But beyond the personal meaning there is something deeper.

Mark presents Jesus as revealing this deeper meaning to an inner group of the disciples, Peter, James, John, and Andrew (XIII: 3), who were the first ones to be summoned as disciples (I: 16–20) and the first ones named in the list of the Twelve (III: 13–18). Here Jesus gives his teaching very much in the manner of a Jewish scribe – sitting being the classic posture for a teacher – and the subject of his teaching, the mystery of the end of the world, was one that, among the scribes, was reserved only for the initiated: the 'wise', not the 'babes'. Similar restrictions on teaching the mysteries were still in force among Christians three centuries later, as we know from evidence about their baptismal instructions.

The mystery revealed to the inner group was that cosmic disasters were about to take place, beginning with minor disasters, mere 'birth-pangs' such as wars, earthquakes, and famines (Mark XIII: 7–8), which are to be followed by the persecution of those who have followed Jesus (verse 13). Then comes unprecedented suffering heralded by the Abomination of Desolation 'standing where it ought not' (verse 14) and the simultaneous eclipse of the sun, moon, and stars (verses 24–5). Only after this will the true Son of Man come and 'gather the elect from the four winds' (verse 27).

The idea of an ultimate period of conflict out of which God brings final victory and salvation was common to Jews of many different persuasions both before and after the lifetime of Jesus, and many interesting parallels can be drawn between teachings on the ultimate conflict and victory, as portrayed in such Jewish writings as the Qumran 'War of the Sons of Light and the Sons of Darkness', and a Christian apocalypse such as the Book of Revelation. Jesus is not simply repeating a standard apocalypse to the group he has gathered, rather he is saying what he, the Son of Man, will be doing (compare Mark II: 10 with XIII: 6 and 26 to see him using the title). Matthew speaks of his disciples linking the 'coming' of Jesus and the end of the age (XXIV: 3). Here is an important side-light on Jesus' kingly or messianic claims: they are to be interpreted in cosmic terms, and not to be confined within the nationalistic arena of Roman-Jewish politics.

Since before the early third century, when it is mentioned in the apocryphal Acts of John, one particular cave on the Mount of Olives had been regarded by Christians as the place where Jesus imparted this teaching to his inner group. The 'mysterious' character of the occasion is emphasized in an early commentary on Matthew's Gospel written by Jerome and probably quoted from Origen, who wrote at the same time as the Acts of John: 'Jesus "sat on the Mount of Olives", where the true light of knowledge was brought into being, "and the disciples" who wished to learn mysteries and have the future revealed "came to him privately". They ask three things: when Jerusalem is to be destroyed, when the Christ will come, and when will be the consummation of the age.'

90 The summit of the Mount of Olives seen from the south-west. The large buildings in the foreground are those of the Carmelite Convent of the Pater Noster. The roofless building attached to them on the left is a restoration of the Church on the Mount of Olives (or Eleona) originally built by Constantine

The cave is one of three holy places chosen by the Emperor Constantine to be the site of a church, no doubt because it was believed to be the setting of the Ascension and (thus) of the Second Coming. The restored church that he built 'On the Mount of Olives' or 'On the Eleona', as the people said in Jerusalem, is shown in Ill. 90. It has been partly rebuilt in this century and is the roofless building attached to the lower end of the group comprising the Carmelite convent. It had a high sanctuary covering the cave, as indicated in Ill. 91, which is based on the reconstruction visible in the photograph. Only the church has

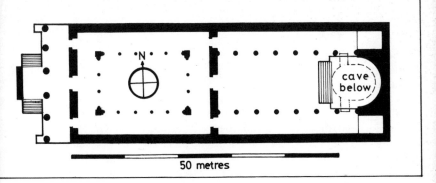

91 Constantine's Church on the Mount of Olives, with its court and porch. The church was built to contain the Cave of Christ's Teaching, which is beneath the sanctuary. The eastern apse, if not as shown, may have protruded from the east wall

92 A sketch-plan of the Cave of Christ's Teaching now enclosed beneath the sanctuary of Constantine's Church on the Mount of Olives. Immediately to its west is a tomb chamber, but this seems to have been blocked off from the cave by a wall as soon as Constantine's Church was built

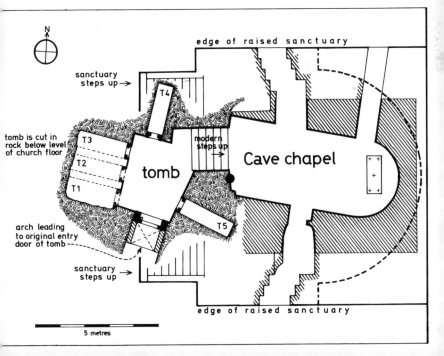

been reconstructed, and not the court. The original western porch, with its steps, stretched as far as the modern road. The remains of the church buildings were constantly being plundered for building stone in the course of the centuries and it is therefore difficult to be sure of the arrangements at the east end. Nor can we say much about the cave itself, of which Ill. 92 is a sketch-plan. The form of the original cave can best be seen in the meticulous drawings by the Dominican Father Vincent, since the remains visible in his day included a good deal more of the rock roof than can now be seen. The small apse in the east end of the cave may well be Constantinian.

The tomb chamber next to the cave was not seen by Father Vincent, who simply shows the wall blocking it on the east and separating it from the cave. When the White Fathers discovered the chapel in 1910 this tomb chamber was still filled with earth. The tomb chamber contains five pairs of tomb shelves, one above the other (T1–5) and may first have been excavated in the second or third centuries A D, when it was beside the cave but not connected with it, as appears from the fact that it had its own entry door leading in from the south. The remains of this door are still to be seen in the tomb chamber. Probably the rearrangement of the cave as a chapel meant that the builders unwittingly broke into the tomb and then had to wall it off. It is hardly likely that this particular chamber was used for burying the bishops of Jerusalem, since it is a crude affair, which obviously existed before Constantine's church. We are told, however, that their tombs were at the church, and therefore they cannot have been far away.

City of Wrath

Convulsions, so Jesus taught, were about to shake the world, and inevitably Jerusalem was to be their epicentre. Nor was the Holy City invulnerable, despite the fact that the Temple of the Lord was there, as had long ago been plain to the prophet Jeremiah (see Jeremiah VII:4). Not one stone of that Temple would be left upon another (Mark XIII:2) because Jerusalem ignored the things that bring peace (Luke XIX:42). So, as Jesus says, 'Your house shall be left unto you desolate' (Matthew XXIII:38): he is addressing Jerusalem, the city which surrounds and regards the great Temple enclosure, the Mountain of the House. God's house there, and the houses of all the great and mighty there, are together doomed.

Luke presumably wrote his Gospel after A D 70, and the Roman siege and pillage of Jerusalem. For him the defeat of the Jewish nation at the hands of the Romans is the fulfilment of the prophecies of destruction that he found in his sources, Mark's Gospel and the collection of material we call Q. Thus where Mark had written, 'When you see the abomination of desolation standing where it ought not (let the reader understand!)' (XIII:14), Luke writes more clearly: 'When you see Jerusalem surrounded by armies, then know that its desolation has come near . . . For these are the days of vengeance . . . for great distress shall be upon the earth, and wrath upon his people (XXI:20–23).

Grave misunderstandings have been caused by this language in the New Testament, and it can only be understood in the light of the Old Testament sources from which so much of it is drawn. Thus 'These are the days of vengeance' is not the description of capricious damage wrought by an enraged God, but the agonized and inevitable response of God whose own covenant people (according to the Gospel writers) have disowned him. The phrase is borrowed from Deuteronomy XXXII: 35: 'I will repay in the day of vengeance, in the hour when their foot shall slip; for the day of their destruction is near, and it stands ready for you.' Or again it recalls the destruction of the impenitent idolaters of Jerusalem pictured by Ezekiel, who are all slain, while those who have sighed and groaned at the evil are spared (IX: 1–11).

These sad themes are part of Israel's own heritage. What the Gospel writers do is to declare that they apply to the Jerusalem of their day because it has refused the very Saviour anointed to redeem it. Their innovation is merely that they apply the ancient warnings to the people of their own day. In the following section we follow Jesus through the final stages of the rejection, which was seen by his followers as having such far-reaching effects.

The Last Supper

The Gospel of John shows Jesus as a life-long frequenter of Jerusalem at the time of feasts. He may have planned to reform and even to transform some aspects of the Judaism of his day, but he is presented as an observant if critical Jew. We should thus expect that it was his intention to keep the Passover on the day accepted by the religious authorities, rather than on the same day as sectarians. According to Mark he ate the Passover meal (XIV: 14), but John implies that his final meal with the Twelve on the night before his crucifixion was not the Passover meal. According to John, that meal was held only on the night following the crucifixion (see John XVIII: 28).

All the Gospel writers agree that Jesus ate a final meal with his disciples on a Thursday night (in our modern phraseology) and was crucified on a Friday. The discrepancy, which amounts in fact to a discrepancy between Mark and John, is that for Mark the Thursday night was the fourteenth day of the month Nisan, and thus the appropriate night for the Passover meal, while for John the Friday was the fourteenth, and the Last Supper as he describes it shows no sign of being a Passover meal.

As has often been pointed out the two traditions convey different theological overtones. For Mark the Passover meal is made the occasion of Jesus's words about the broken bread, which was in some prophetic sense his body, and the shared cup of wine, which was his blood. The traditional Jewish celebration is transposed into a new context of thought. For John, the Last Supper is accompanied by a last example of humility and service, when Jesus washes the feet of the disciples. The Passover theme for John, then, is probably implied by the timing of events on the Friday, since Jesus, the Lamb of God (a phrase used earlier in the Gospel: John I: 29, 36), is slain on the Cross at the very time when the Passover lambs were being slain in the Temple. Have we any hope of telling which of the two time-schemes is historically accurate? The consensus of scholars at present seems to be in favour of John, but to the present writer it seems that the answer is far from obvious. Nor as a matter of fact are we all clear about the location of the guest room where the Last Supper was held. Indeed the disciples themselves did not know the place until they were led to it by the man carrying a pitcher of water (Mark XIV: 13). Hence we may assume that the Galilean and his disciples borrowed the room for this one occasion, and that it has nothing to do with houses or rooms in Jerusalem which are mentioned later in the New Testament. The memory of the Last Supper is now celebrated in the Cenacle on Mount Sion, but it is only a secondary commemoration at that site, as we shall be seeing below.

Gethsemane

When Jesus sent Peter and John to look for the man with the pitcher of water, who would guide them to the upper room of the Last Supper, he sent them 'into the city' (Luke XXII: 10). Most probably the supper was held somewhere within the city walls, but when it was over they went out 'across the Kidron' (John XVIII: 1), 'onto the Mount of Olives' (Mark XIV: 26). Gethsemane, where they were going, was a 'habitual' rendezvous (Luke XXII: 39) and 'Jesus had often met there with his disciples' (John XVIII: 2). We know that on the night after the triumphal entry Jesus was in Bethany (Mark XI: 11–12) and that later on he was at an evening meal there in the house of Simon the Leper (XIV: 3). So it seems that he stayed at least for some nights in Bethany. But it is also possible that there was enough shelter in the garden for him to sleep there if he wished. Shelter would certainly have been needed in April. John tells us that it was cold (XVIII: 18) and at that time of year there can still be heavy falls of rain.

The account by Mark, closely followed by that of Matthew, now describes how Jesus withdraws with Peter, James, and John, and admits to them that his 'soul is heavy' (words from Psalm XLIII: 5). Next he prays with total concentration to God asking that if possible he be spared the ordeal ahead: 'Take this cup away from me – yet not what I want but what you want' (Mark XIV: 36). But this concentration and vigilance is not shared by the disciples, whom he repeatedly finds asleep (XIV: 37, 40, 41). The pathos of this episode is deepened by Luke, who describes him sweating as he prays, with the sweat dripping to the ground like drops of blood, and says that the disciples were 'sleeping for sorrow' (XXII: 41–45). John, however, avoids all pathos, saying nothing of Jesus' prayer to be spared, and lays the whole stress on Jesus' strength in this time of crisis.

Next, all the Gospel writers describe the arrival of Judas, who comes and greets Jesus in the manner still commonly used by pupils for the rabbis or sheikhs who are their teachers: with a kiss. Though there was nothing out of the ordinary in the manner of greeting, Luke presents Jesus as grieved or angered that it should be used as part of Judas' betrayal (XXII: 48). According to Mark, Judas has with him the Temple police, who were Levites, officially despatched by the Sanhedrin, for this is surely the group intended by the phrase 'the chief priests and the scribes and the elders' (XIV: 43). Luke indeed tells us that some of the chief priests, chief officers (*strategoi*), and priests came in person (XXII: 52). So Jesus is arrested.

None of the four Gospels records any further fear or hesitation on Jesus' part. For Mark, Matthew, and Luke the prayer in Gethsemane has resolved his apprehensions. And John (here surely reacting against Mark's account of the Gethsemane prayer, and wishing to show the other side of its meaning) describes Jesus as saying 'This is a cup my Father has given me. Shouldn't I drink it?' (XVIII: 11). Jesus challenges his captors by asking why they had to come out after him at night, as if they were chasing a burglar? Why did they need to carry arms? Would it not have been perfectly simple to come and arrest him in the Temple when he was teaching? The party sent to arrest him knew the answer only too well. The 'multitude who heard him gladly' (Mark XII: 37) would have been outraged. He had many supporters – 'All the world has gone after him' (John XII: 19) – and the only chance of arresting him was to choose a time when he would not be accompanied by a crowd. Jesus gives yet another expression of his resolve by rejecting Peter's quixotic effort to defend him by force of arms (John XVIII: 11).

Where Mark and those who follow his presentation speak of the party sent to arrest Jesus as if it was the Sanhedrin or its servants, John speaks of a party made up of two groups, one of which might be Roman. He speaks of 'the military unit' (*speira*) under its commander (*chiliarchos*) on the one hand, and on the other hand of the 'officers' of the high priests and Pharisees, or (as he also calls them) of 'the Jews'

(XVIII: 3, 12). If 'the military unit' were indeed Roman then there would already be collusion between Pilate and the Jewish authorities. In this case the question Pilate first asks Jesus when he sees him, 'Are you the King of the Jews?' (John XVIII: 33), is the question that he and the high priests have agreed will form the final reason for Jesus' execution, and Pilate's subsequent attempts to secure Jesus' release are an attempt to go back on a prior agreement with the Jewish establishment. But as we have seen it was not uncommon to use Roman and Greek technical terms in describing Semitic institutions, and it is most likely that 'the military unit' is simply the Levite police. In this case there need have been no collusion, and Pilate's first question to Jesus would be based simply on his familiarity with Jesus as a popular figure. This interpretation would certainly fit with Mark's presentation of the question (XV: 2), where it seems to be a private question on the tip of Pilate's tongue, which he wants answered before he proceeds to hear the official charges.

Where was Jesus arrested? The 'place' (Mark XIV: 32) or 'orchard' (John XVIII: 1) of Gethsemane sounds hardly the kind of place that would leave identifiable archaeological remains. But its place-name has never gone out of use, and its general area is not in doubt. It is shown in Ill. 93, which includes the floor of the Kidron Valley. In Greek the word 'Brook', which describes the Kidron, means 'winter stream', and where the bed of the brook can be seen it is dry for most of the year. But in the area shown in our photograph the stream has been enclosed in an underground channel and therefore cannot be seen. In fact it is running diagonally across from the middle of the top of the picture, then parallel to the far wall of the Virgin's Tomb (the large building in the middle of the picture with the flat roof) and about ten metres (about 31 feet) to its left. It passes under the road bridge very near the point where the white car is crossing and then it continues across to the area of the garden in the bottom left of the picture. Since the Kidron has always been and still is a natural drain for the city area of Jerusalem it is certainly in the public interest that parts of it have been covered, even though it makes the study of the area slightly less easy.

93 (overleaf) The area of Gethsemane seen from the south. The Church of the Agony (or Church of All Nations) is in the foreground and the Cave of Gethsemane is beneath the D-shaped roof (arrow). The Tomb of the Virgin is to the left (arrow)

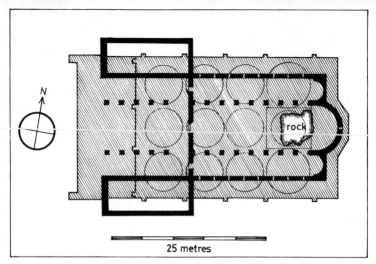

94 *The shaded area is that of the modern Church of All Nations, which includes the site of the Byzantine Church of the Agony (the plan of which is shown in black). The focal point of both churches is the rock on which tradition said Jesus had knelt to pray*

The name Gethsemane (meaning 'oil-press') is probably applied to the area immediately surrounding the Church of the Agony and the Virgin's Tomb, and there is no reason to doubt that Jesus was indeed arrested somewhere in the area shown in the photograph. But there are no solid grounds for more precision about the place of the prayer of agony and the arrest. The rock on which, according to tradition, Jesus knelt to pray, was surrounded in about 380 by a church, whose plan is shown in black in Ill. 94, and can still be seen in the present church (shown by the shaded area). But it is hardly likely that the exact place of the prayer would have been remembered, and there is nothing of special note about the rock.

Immediately beyond the Church of the Agony is a formal garden maintained by the Franciscans and containing some venerable olive trees. Of these some may be as much as a thousand years old, but it is unlikely they could survive for much longer. Near the Virgin's Tomb and to its right can be seen a D-shaped roof that has a circular skylight protruding from it. This, as appears in Ill. 95, is the roof of a cave that has provided the setting for various Christian commemorations, including Jesus' arrest. It was also regarded as a suitable place in which he might have lodged for the night. Beneath the cave are some

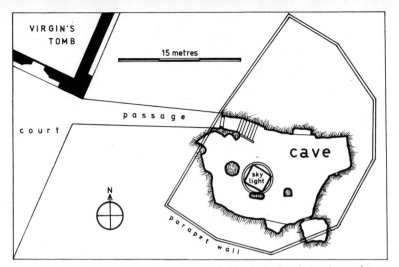

95 The Gethsemane Cave near the Virgin's Tomb. In Jesus' time it may have been used as a place where olives were processed

channels and in its roof is a hole (now covered by a skylight). Its purposes before the fourth century A D, when it began to be used for burials, may have included use as a cistern and perhaps even the processing of olives.

The Trial

During April sunset comes to Jerusalem at about 6.00 p.m. If we imagine the Last Supper as beginning at that moment it can be assumed to have finished around 9.00 p.m. The walk across the Kidron Valley to Gethsemane would take at least a quarter of an hour and the prayer in Gethsemane perhaps an hour and a half. It is not likely therefore that the police arrested Jesus before 10.30 p.m., and it would probably be past 11.00 p.m. by the time Jesus was delivered at the house of Caiaphas.

One dimension of Jesus' trial thus becomes clear. Whatever the high priest may have wished to do with Jesus between 11.00 p.m. and dawn – say 5.30 a.m. – he could not formally try him until daybreak. The Mishnah lays it down that 'In capital cases they hold the trial during the daytime, and the verdict must also be reached during the daytime' (*Sanhedrin* 4:1), and this is probably a rule of long standing that would have been in force in Jesus' time. Unfortunately the Mishnah also tells us in the same passage that trials may not be held on the eve of a Sabbath or the eve of a festival day (as Jesus' trial was), and that a verdict of conviction cannot be given until the day after the trial (whereas Jesus' trial and conviction were on the same day). If all these rules were in force in Jesus' time then his trial was technically irregular. But such technicalities are far less important than the basic question: had the judges any interest in the prisoner? As soon as we seek the answer in the Gospels (which of course have their own strong bias in Jesus' favour) we find that the members of the court were already involved in a plot to kill him. Caiaphas, who as high priest was president of the court, had said that it would be useful if 'one man should die for the people', and 'from that day on they [the members of the Sanhedrin] took counsel how they might put him to death' (John XI: 47, 50, 53). For John, then, the trial is a frame-up. How is it presented by the other Gospel writers? Mark, followed by Matthew and Luke, presents Jesus as foreseeing that 'the elders and the chief priests and the scribes', that is to say, the Sanhedrin, would 'reject' Jesus and that he would 'be killed' (Mark VIII: 31, IX: 31, X: 33–34). The chief priests and scribes were seeking how to arrest him by stealth and kill him (XIV: 1). Legal niceties in the trial of Jesus are therefore of little interest to the Gospel writers, since their main point is that the authorities are already determined to condemn Jesus to death before they conduct his trial.

Unless Pilate was in collusion with the Jewish authorities the trial had to be conducted in such a way by the Sanhedrin that it appeared to follow normal procedure, for Pilate alone could pronounce sentence of death. The Sanhedrin had lost this power after Archelaus had been deposed in AD 6, and it was then reserved to the Roman governor, which is the implication of Josephus' statement that the first governor was sent to Judaea 'with power extending as far as the infliction of the death penalty' (*War* 2:117). Thus the Sanhedrin, if it wished Jesus to be executed, was obliged to bring him to be condemned to death by the prefect Pilate.

We have seen that Caiaphas' time-table for the morning was awkward. Having arrested Jesus he could take no official action against him for perhaps six hours. But there was another problem which was equally difficult. The secret arrest of Jesus would not become public knowledge until some hours of daylight had gone by, but the longer the execution was delayed, the more likelihood there would be of demonstrations or appeals in Jesus' favour. Not only did Caiaphas have to put off the formal trial till daybreak, but he had to ensure that the trial should be as rapid as possible, so that he could take the prisoner before Pilate and have him executed the same day. This meant that the Sanhedrin had to work fast, since Pilate, though he was probably available to the public from dawn, would, like other Roman officials, retire into his private life at about 11.00 a.m.

Caiaphas therefore had to collect a quorum of the Sanhedrin by daybreak (first light at 4.30 a.m. or sunrise at 5.30). This meeting had to condemn Jesus on charges which Pilate could recognize as deserving the death penalty, and, since the prefect must not be given the opportunity to adjourn the hearing, it should start in his Praetorium not later than about 10.00 a.m. or, in the parlance of the period, halfway through the fifth hour. If everything went according to plan Jesus could be executed soon after 11.00 a.m.

Night Work

As much preparatory work as possible had to be done during the night: in particular a committee of Sanhedrin members needed to work on the charges against the prisoner so that the quorum could reach its decision soon after dawn. We may suppose that the committee met in the house of the high priest Caiaphas (Mark XIV: 53, Luke XXII: 54, and John XVIII: 15). John tells us that the director of the first enquiry was not in fact the high priest, but Annas, his father-in-law and predecessor. Special arrangements made for the night shift may be indicated by the lighting of a brazier in the courtyard (John XVIII: 18, Mark XIV: 67).

We have no reliable information about the location of this house, though we may reasonably guess that it was somewhere in the Upper City, like that of the Ananus who was high priest in AD 47–55 (Josephus, *War* 2:426). Efforts have been made to show that the remains on the site of the Church of St Peter in Gallicantu must have been the house. Partly this was because a set of weights found there were of a different standard from other weights, and it was assumed that this was so because they conformed with a special Temple

96 (overleaf) The Church of St Peter in Gallicantu (arrow), down the slopes of Mt Sion on the left foreground, seen from the east. In early tradition a 'house of Caiaphas' was shown to pilgrims at some place nearer to the summit of the hill, and to the site of the modern Church of the Dormition (arrow) with its conical roof

standard. But since this discovery (well before the First World War) many other sets of weights have been found, few of them weighing the same, and no argument can be based on them. Similarly there is no agreement on the meaning of an inscription found there, now obliterated, which included the word 'Corban'. Since the fourth century A D Church tradition has always placed the house of Caiaphas higher up and nearer Holy Sion, in the position shown in Ill. 113, but since our earliest source for this tradition also speaks of a 'house of Pilate' in an entirely wrong position we cannot be confident that in this case the tradition is reliable.

Wherever Caiaphas' house may have been (and in Ill. 100 we place it somewhere in the Mount Sion area for want of other suggestions) it was not the Chamber of Hewn Stone in which we are told the Sanhedrin had to hold its official meetings. That, we have suggested, was in or near the Temple area. What then do we know of the unofficial preliminary meeting now taking place in Caiaphas' house? The high priest's purpose, according to Mark (who tells us that *all* the officials were there, XIV:53, 55), was to seek evidence against Jesus which would be sufficient to obtain a death sentence (XIV:55). John may be describing a similarly motivated interrogation when he tells us how Annas asked Jesus about his 'disciples and his teaching', but his object is not at this point (XVIII:19) similar enough to allow us to make firm comparisons. It is clear in all the Gospels that the final result of the Jewish interrogations was a charge that Jesus claimed to be Son of God. This claim is explicit in Mark XIV:62 coming from the lips of Jesus himself, but it is alleged by the accusers in the other accounts (see Matthew XXVI:63, Luke XXII:70 and John XIX:7). Such a claim was treated as blasphemy (thus, according to Numbers XV:30, meriting death) and the Mishnah requires that when blasphemy was proved the judges were to respond with the gesture of standing up and rending their garments (*Sanhedrin* 7:5), 'and they may not mend them again'.

No doubt the formulation of this charge was part of the night committee's work. But, since Pilate might not acknowledge it as serious enough to deserve death, an alternative tactic seems to have been used – that in case of doubt they should mention Jesus' political claim: to be a king (John XIX:12).

When the committee had finished interviewing Jesus he was available for the insults which 'certain persons' (Mark XIV:65) or the committee members (Matthew XXVI:67) or, better, 'the men who were guarding Jesus' (Luke XXII:63) inflicted on him when they blindfolded and beat him. At the same time the cocks were crowing, to the consternation of Peter, but cocks can crow long before dawn, and we cannot estimate the lapse of time.

At daybreak we may envisage Jesus already waiting near the Chamber of Hewn Stone, perhaps watching his judges assemble, and then being taken before them. This was the formal session of the Sanhedrin (Luke XXII:66), sitting under the presidency of Caiaphas (John XVIII:24), which 'at once reached a decision' (the meaning of Mark XV:1 according to some translators) or at least 'at once held a council meeting'. It makes little difference which. For the result of this purely formal meeting is to ratify the charge formulated by the night committee, and make their proposal into an official act of the Sanhedrin so that Jesus can be taken as a condemned man to Pilate.

The Hearing By Pilate

When a Roman was appointed to govern a province he was invested with full authority to administer his territory, exercise judicial functions, give orders for the defence of the province and maintain internal law and order. He was extremely powerful, and the provincial subjects of the empire had no automatic right of appeal against him. Hence Pilate in judging Jesus was free himself to decide both on the innocence or guilt of the accused and on the appropriate sentence. And he was of course invested with authority to inflict the death penalty. He was therefore entirely free to adopt or reject the Sanhedrin's decision as he wished, and also to consult with any one he wished (such as Herod Antipas) or to deal with the case by himself.

This great power was in the hands of a man for whom the Jews had little respect. Philo in his *Delegation to Gaius* (Chapter 38) complains that Pilate was characterized by 'venality, violence, robbery, ill-treatment, insult, ceaseless executions without trial, and by irrational and terrible cruelty'. His final misdemeanour as governor was a massacre of Samaritans in AD 36 for which he was sent back to Rome by Vitellius. All this had been implicit in Jesus' warning that the Son of Man, when he had been condemned to death by the chief priests and the scribes, would be handed over to foreigners (Mark X:33).

We know from various scraps of information about other Roman prefects of Judaea that while normally they lived in Caesarea, they also had an official residence, or 'praetorium', in Jerusalem. A praetorium of Herod in Caesarea is mentioned in Acts XXIII:35. In Jerusalem Herod the Great had built two buildings we might call palaces. One

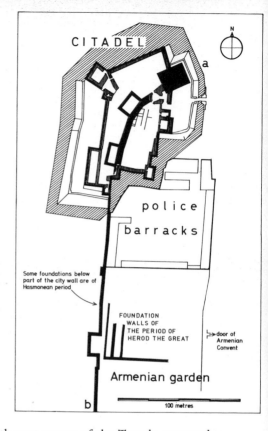

97 *The medieval Citadel and the area to the south contain all or at any rate most of the remains of the royal Palace of Herod the Great. Apart from the Herodian tower at the north-east end of the Citadel the remains so far discovered are mostly foundations*

98 *(opposite) The excavations inside the Citadel show the line of the Herodian city wall (arrow) with its towers*

was the Antonia at the north-west corner of the Temple area; and Josephus, who says that it was 'like a palace' (*War* V: 241), may mean that though it was not really a palace it was unusually impressive for a fort. The other was 'the upper palace' in the Upper City (*War* II: 429) which was, as we have seen, one of the elaborate buildings erected during the building campaign that followed the famine of 25–24 BC. Recent archaeological work by Professor Ruth Amiran and Dr Magen Broshi has shown that the general line of the wall (see Ill. 97, a–b) is to be dated (by what has so far been examined of the foundations) to the period of the Hasmonean kings, and that the foundations shown inside this wall by the second tower from the top – also visible in the centre of Ill. 98 – were constructed during the reign of Herod the Great. These foundations are very deep, and enabled the ground floor of Herod's Palace to be raised three or four metres higher than that of the Hasmonean buildings which had previously occupied the site. The

walls that were found in the Armenian Garden, the site of the new Manoogian Seminary, though on a different scale, were also intended as supports for part of the platform of Herod's Palace. These discoveries show that the Palace with its grounds was of considerable size. Earlier examinations by C. N. Johns strongly suggest that the large tower (a) on its solid masonry base, which was certainly Herod's, is the one he named Phasael in memory of his brother. But of the arrangement of the Palace and its two remarkable towers, Hippicus and Mariamme, we are otherwise totally ignorant apart from the descriptions by Josephus.

Even if it is correct to think of the Antonia as being a palace then we should have little difficulty in deciding which of the two was chosen as the Roman prefect's residence, or praetorium, after the collapse of the Herods. The Antonia was cramped and Herod had redeveloped it near the beginning of his career as a builder. Herod's Palace, properly so called, was built twelve years later and must have incorporated the results of a great deal of architectural experience. Philo in his *Delegation to Gaius* (Chapter 38) tells us plainly that on the occasion of a Jewish feast Pilate was residing in 'Herod's Palace in the Holy City', which he describes as 'the residence of the prefects', and Gessius Florus, prefect from A D 64, came to reside 'in the Palace' in May A D 66 on the eve of the first Jewish-Roman War. Thus we may understand the language of Mark XV: 16 to mean that at the end of his trial the soldiers led Jesus 'inside the Palace, that is, the Praetorium'.

Mark does not tell us precisely where in the Palace Jesus was tried by Pilate. Matthew XXVII: 19, however, does tell us that Pilate was sitting on a *bema*, or, as we might call it, platform, and Luke presents the whole trial as taking place in the presence of the chief priests and the crowds (XXIII: 4). How was this possible? The answer seems to be that the trial was conducted out of doors, and John explains it by saying that Jesus' accusers did not go inside the Praetorium 'in order that they should not be made unclean, but should eat the Passover' (XVIII: 28). There is a slight doubt whether this reason was technically correct, since it would, perhaps, have been possible to undergo ritual cleansing before sunset, when the day of the Passover feast began. Suffice it to note that part of John's intention may have been to explain a trial out of doors.

We should, therefore, picture the *bema*, or platform, mentioned by Matthew as standing in the open air. John presents the trial as occurring outside, in episodes which are interspersed by private interviews between Pilate and Jesus inside the Palace. Pilate's final

99 The Herodian masonry of the north-east tower of the Citadel is clearly visible from the west. It stands on a solid masonry base. This was probably the tower that Herod named after his brother Phasael, since its measurements are fairly close to those of that tower as reported by Josephus

sentence is delivered from a seat 'in the place called *Lithostroton*, but in Hebrew Gabbatha' (XIX:13) – the two words, as John seems to imply, have different meanings. Lithostroton means 'paved place', and Gabbatha means 'raised place'. We may therefore guess that the regular procedure at the Palace was to use a raised outdoor paved area near by, on which the resident Palace official set up a platform for his public appearances. This guess is made considerably more probable by our knowledge that Josephus tells us of two prefects who addressed angry crowds in Jerusalem from a platform: Pilate in about AD 30 and Florus in AD 66 (*War* 2:175–76, 301, 308).

At some point in his trial Jesus was dressed as a king and mocked. Mark and Matthew say that this was done by the Roman soldiers after the official flogging, thus making Pilate flog Jesus – apparently before he decided that Jesus was to be crucified. Possibly the best memory of the mockery is that preserved for us by Luke, who says that Jesus was mocked not by Pilate's but by Herod Antipas' soldiers (Luke XXIII: 11). Since Luke presents Jesus as having had little respect for Antipas, calling him 'that fox' (XIII: 32), we may perhaps be intended to see Herod's revenge in the mockery. The fact that a hearing before Herod Antipas is mentioned only in Luke's Gospel does not mean that it is unhistorical.

If such a hearing was held, where would Herod Antipas' palace have been? Probably he lived in the old palace of the Hasmoneans, which Josephus tells us overlooked the Xystus (*War* 2:344), the Xystus being in all probability an open space reaching to the western end of the bridge leading into the Temple area. This is shown near No. 2 in Ill. 100. We know that in Byzantine times a Church of St Sophia stood in this vicinity, which was then believed to have been the Praetorium where Pilate had Jesus flogged. It has been suggested that this site might in fact have been chosen because it was the Hasmonean palace. Alternatively, it may have been chosen because by the date of Jesus' trial this site was the *boulē*, or *bouleutērion*, where the Sanhedrin held its official meetings. Thus the name 'Chamber of Hewn Stone' mentioned at the meeting-place in the Mishnah (e.g. *Sanhedrin* 11:2, *Middoth* 5:4), and there regarded as being inside the Temple may, in fact, have only been given the name when the new council 'chamber' was built next to the 'Area of Hewn Stone', or 'Xystus'. The Babylonian Talmud states that the Sanhedrin 'was exiled' from the Chamber of Hewn Stone to a bazaar 'forty years' before the destruction of Jerusalem (B.Talmud *A. Zar*. 8b). This means that the Sanhedrin moved its meeting-place at about the time of Jesus' trial, but most likely a little later, probably from a chamber by the main Temple building to the new Chamber 'of' or 'at' the Xystus. The position of the Xystus appears on the right of Ill. 64 and was probably at a site about 2.5 cm to the left of the arrow.

Who's To Blame?

A standard ingredient in Christian attacks on Jews has been the accusation that they killed Jesus. Who in fact was to blame for his death? This question was already more than half answered before the trial began if, as we have seen, Jesus is caught up in a conflict with the establishment, concretely represented by the Jerusalem Sanhedrin, for we know that this body that tried him also wished to secure his death. If the Gospel writers are correct in this analysis then the formalities of the trial are of comparatively little importance, since they are simply being used as means to an end. None the less let us review them.

The intention on the part of the establishment to kill Jesus is expressed by Mark (XI:18) and Luke (XIX:47) in passages that contrast the official desire to remove Jesus and the fear of his supporters. Matthew slightly expands this passage, but makes it equally clear that the intention of the 'chief priests and elders of the people' is to 'arrest Jesus by stealth and kill him', and John makes precisely the same point at greater length and in greater depth (XI:47–57).

The account of the trial before the Sanhedrin thus involves a preliminary stage in which a committee asks itself what charge will suitably require a death sentence. Then the Sanhedrin as a whole finds Jesus guilty on this charge and passes him over to the authority competent to execute the sentence.

Pilate is told the charges, but is unable to see that Jesus has done serious wrong. 'What evil has he done?' he asks (Mark XV:14). But the crowd, prompted by the chief priests (Mark XV:11), simply cries out for him to be crucified. Pilate gives way to their request, though he has 'found in him nothing worthy of death' (Luke XXIII:22), and symbolizes his refusal to accept responsibility for Jesus' death by washing his hands (Matthew XXVII:24). This contemptible gesture is treated as such by the crowds who reply 'His blood be on us and our children' or, as we might paraphrase it, 'You're the Roman prefect, with power to condemn him to death. If you won't take the responsibility, we will!' So Jesus is handed over to the Roman soldiers to have his sentence carried out. Eventually the title on the cross said 'The King of the Jews'. Who then is to blame?

Judas is held partly responsible by Matthew and Luke, each of whom describes his end (Matthew XXVII:3–10, Acts I:16–20) as a death befitting the perpetrator of a great sin. The Sanhedrin of the day is shown as plotting, and eventually securing, Jesus' death by manipulating its judicial process, swaying the crowd, and, finally, by cowing Pilate into giving way to its demand. This Sanhedrin is therefore the prime mover and, as we have seen, a great deal of the dynamic of the Gospels arises out of the conflict between this body and Jesus. Lastly Pilate also is to blame, for he is presented as handing over to crucifixion a prisoner whom he regarded as innocent. Neither Jews nor Romans are exonerated, and all contributed to the tragedy.

The Gospel-tragedy is presented in the way it is in order to persuade the Jews and Romans of other days and in other places to heed the work of Jesus and to put their faith to him and – in the familiar words of Psalm LXXVIII:8 – 'Not to be as their forefathers, a faithless and stubborn generation'. The Gospels by their Passion-narratives offer a woeful scene of human hatred, vindictiveness, wilful ignorance, and cowardice. It has implications for any human being who gives way to such instincts and emotions. But to the present writer it seems that past attempts by Christians to interpret the Passion in such a way as to condemn modern Jews exemplify the very attitudes the Passion-narratives were designed to challenge. Christians may believe that Jews brought about the crucifixion. But they also believe in the Jew who was crucified.

Finding the Way of the Cross

From the Praetorium the Roman soldiers took Jesus out to crucify him at Golgotha. This episode has become so hallowed by the devotion known internationally as the 'Stations of the Cross' that we cannot examine it adequately without first pausing to examine this traditional exercise.

In the fourth century A D we hear of two Holy Week processions. One was held on Palm Sunday to commemorate Jesus' triumphal entry into Jerusalem and the other on the night of Thursday to commemorate some of the events leading up to the trial of Jesus. But we hear of no procession to commemorate the 'Way of the Cross' until the thirteenth century. Ill. 100 shows how this 'Way of the Cross' went from 'Praetorium 3' or, as we have earlier described it, the Antonia, which was one of the two sites treated as the Praetorium during the Middle Ages. Not only does the early evidence show that Pilate's Praetorium was in fact at the Palace ('Praetorium 1'), but the Byzantine topography of the city treated not the Antonia but St Sophia (Ill. 100, 'Praetorium 2') as the place of Pilate's house. The Crusader topography thus has no links with a continuous tradition, and need not be taken too seriously. In fact if our present argument for the authenticity of 'Praetorium 1' is correct then the medieval 'Way of the Cross', running towards Golgotha from 'Praetorium 3', runs in the opposite direction from the one it should.

We have already examined the two sites that are proposed as the house of Caiaphas (in Ill. 100 'a' is the traditional site which has some chance of being authentic but has not so far been excavated, and 'b' is St Peter in Gallicantu). We have now seen three of the sites believed to have been the Praetorium, of which '1' is the only one that is probable.

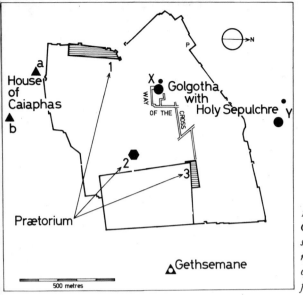

100 The Way of the Cross in modern Jerusalem, with some alternative sites for the events of Jesus' trial and crucifixion

We also have two sites for Golgotha, which at present hold the field: 'Golgotha X', which is at the traditional Holy Sepulchre Church, and 'Golgotha Y', which is outside the walled city. At both the visitor is shown a place of the crucifixion and a nearby tomb. Has either of these sites any claim to authenticity? And what does the Bible tell us about the sites of the crucifixion and burial?

According to John, the tomb where Jesus' body was buried was in a garden (or orchard) 'in the place where he was crucified' (XIX:41). It was near by (XIX:42), and we must thus understand Golgotha as being the name of a single site both of the cross and of the tomb. Despite the long-standing tradition that Golgotha was a hill – 'a green hill far away' in the words of Mrs Alexander – the Gospels all speak of it simply as a 'place'. But Mrs Alexander is clearly right when she says that it was 'without a city wall'. Not only was it impossible to bury any one inside a city, but John says Jesus 'went out' to Golgotha (XIX:17), surely implying that 'Jesus suffered outside the gate' (Hebrews XIII:12). But both 'Golgotha Y' and 'Golgotha X' were outside the wall before its extension in AD 44 when Herod Agrippa I probably brought the city boundary more or less to the line between the word 'Sepulchre' and the projection marked 'P' on Ill. 100. The position of 'Golgotha X' may have related to the wall in the way suggested in Ill. 104, but it must be remembered that the line of the

145

wall we show is pure guesswork, and may well be wrong. We may be encouraged by the discovery at both 'Golgotha X' and 'Y' of tombs of a type used in Jesus' time. But even these are hardly conclusive, because their style shows only that they could have been made some time between about 200 BC and AD 200. Thus they might already have been emptied by Herod the Great, and the areas brought into the city boundary before the date of Jesus' crucifixion and burial.

What leads us to suppose that 'Golgotha Y' is to be identified with the place of a skull? Modern guides usually point out the caves on its southern cliff near the one known since the sixteenth century as 'Jeremiah's Grotto', and suggest that the reason for the description 'Place of a Skull' is the face the visitor is supposed to see in the cliff near the caves. But this rock formation has changed even within living memory, and it is for quite another reason that the hill was adopted as a candidate for Golgotha by General Charles Gordon. His reasons appear in the posthumous article from the Palestine Exploration Fund's *Quarterly Statement*, 1885, reprinted on pp. 198–9, and the present author neither finds them convincing nor knows of any other reason for supposing that the hill in question was known as Golgotha in the time of Jesus. If the hill was Golgotha then the nearby Garden Tomb, purchased in 1894, might be that in which Christ had been buried, as might several of the other ancient tombs in the vicinity. But if there is no special reason for believing the hill to be Golgotha, then there is no special reason for believing in the authenticity of the tomb.

'Golgotha Y' and the Garden Tomb have been shown to visitors for less than a century, but 'Golgotha X', or at least its nearby tomb, was first pointed out probably before AD 135, and has certainly been regarded as the place of Jesus' burial since its recovery by the Emperor Constantine in about AD 325. Its history seems to be as follows: we know from the Gospels and especially from that of John that Jesus was buried in a rock-tomb, which must, by the Jewish custom of the time, have been outside the city wall. Since this burial took place in about AD 30, this need not mean that the tomb is outside the present-day city wall, for Jerusalem was enlarged in AD 44 by Herod Agrippa I and only at this time was 'Golgotha X', with its tomb, probably included within the walls of the city. Nearly a century later the Emperor Hadrian built a temple over the site of the tomb, which was probably dedicated to Jupiter, Juno, and Minerva (who are shown on one of the city's contemporary coins) with a statue of Venus near by. Eighty or ninety years after this official Roman temple was built practically no Christians were left who had known it as it was before.

101 'Gordon's Calvary' is usually said to have been taken to resemble a skull because of the face formed by the two small caves with the nose-like piece of rock between them. But General Gordon identified the hill with Calvary for an entirely different reason

Two centuries later, or to be exact, in AD 325, no living eye had seen what was beneath the temple. Then, as Eusebius tells us in his *Life of Constantine* (3:25–40), the Christian Emperor decided to 'display the most blessed place of the Saviour's resurrection in a worthy and conspicuous manner' and to build a church there. The rock-tomb, or 'divine cave' as Eusebius calls it, had been covered up by soil, which formed the basis for pavements in the sanctuary of the Roman gods. And when this foundation soil was removed the tomb 'came into view'.

Eusebius' account of the discovery is the only one we have from that period. It has the merit of being written by an eye-witness of the site only a dozen or so years after the event described. But it is part of a biography written to flatter the Emperor and often uses phrases that sound unattractively obsequious to modern ears. Moreover it is describing a Christian Emperor's decision to destroy a temple of idols and replace it with a church. Yet the account rings true for the present writer for three main reasons. Firstly we have, as we shall see later on, various indications that Christians cared about 'holy places' before the reign of Constantine. Therefore we may be sure that if the Christian community in the generation following Jesus' death knew Golgotha, as is very likely, they would probably have handed this knowledge on. Secondly, the site that Constantine was arranging to excavate was well

102 The tomb chamber 18 metres (60 feet) west of the site of the Holy Sepulchre agrees well with the prescriptions of the Mishnah, and was probably in use before A D 44. After that it was emptied, since the area was enclosed within the city wall, and later sliced in half by a wall of the rotunda of the fourth-century Church of the Resurrection

inside the city by his time, and if there had been no firm tradition to the position of Golgotha he would surely have looked for it somewhere outside the walls of his own day. Thirdly, the site had once, as we have seen, been a tomb area, because we can still see there, 18 metres (60 feet) from the place of Jesus' tomb, the remains of a rock-tomb of a type used by Jews between 200 BC and AD 200. Since this subsidiary tomb is never mentioned in the Byzantine period and was evidently not being venerated then, we know that it was pre-Constantinian, and therefore also pre-Hadrianic.

This account falls very far short of proving that 'Golgotha X' is the right place. But it does enable us to say that in our present state of knowledge this site, occupied by the traditional Church of the Holy

103 The rock in the Church of the Holy Sepulchre known as Calvary, seen from the north. It is about 4 metres (about 12 feet) square, and Eusebius, who first describes the site, does not say that he regarded it as the Calvary on which Jesus suffered.

Sepulchre, is the only one which can with any probability be regarded as the place in which Jesus was buried. So if we are to look for Golgotha we must look for it at that church, however much the buildings there may have obliterated the original garden, and disguised the rock-tomb and the place where the crosses were set up.

Eusebius, to the frustration of his readers, speaks of the tomb, but says nothing about the place of the crucifixion. A strange block of living rock, visible through the glass in Ill. 103, still exists on the site where, as we know from other fourth-century descriptions, the crucifixion was recalled by setting up a cross and by various processions and acts of prayer. Eusebius, however, who describes the site at length, does not seem to have believed that this rock was the

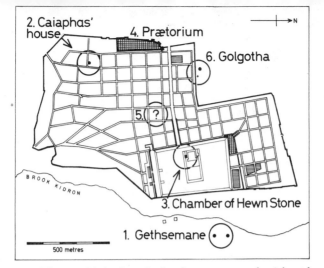

104 The most likely places for Jesus' movements on the night and morning before his crucifixion. No. 5 is the approximate position of the palace used by Herod Antipas, according to Josephus

actual spot where Jesus had hung on the cross, though this claim was already being made when he wrote.

Thus the Way of the Cross was probably a short journey from 'Praetorium 1' to the site of the Holy Sepulchre. These two buildings appear clearly in Ill. 105, the Praetorium being the Citadel, the castle to the right of the Jaffa Gate, and Golgotha the site covered by the church with the two domes just beyond it and to the left. The distance between the two as the crow flies is about 300 metres (considerably less than a quarter of a mile).

In describing this journey the four Gospels select different points of attention. John omits the information that Simon the Cyrenaean helped Jesus carry his cross, which appears in the other three Gospels. Emphasizing as he does the mastery of Jesus over his situation, he says that 'he went out carrying the cross for himself' (XIX:17). In two passages in the *Mostellaria*, a Roman comedy written by Plautus two centuries before Jesus' crucifixion, it is said that one person being executed is to 'carry the crossbar [*patibulum*] through the city' and then 'be attached to the upright stake [*crux*]'. If this was regular practice in the Jerusalem of Jesus' day we ought therefore to picture him as carrying the 'stretcher' or 'crossbar' to the place where the upright stake was already fixed (we presume permanently). It is possible, however, that Jesus had to carry the whole cross himself, and in this case it would hardly be surprising if he soon needed help. That Simon of Cyrene was forced to provide help is hardly questionable, since he is identified by his place of origin and by the names of his sons (see Mark XV: 21). Simon is said to have met Jesus 'as he was coming in from a field'. The soldiers may have seen him as he came in through the Jaffa Gate, but since we have no information about other gates which may have been nearby (such as the Gennath, or 'Gardens', Gate mentioned by Josephus in *War* 5: 146) we cannot be sure. Luke tells us also of Jesus' warning to the women of Jerusalem that if things are bad now they will be far worse before long (XXIII: 31: presumably when the prophecy of Zechariah XII: 2*ff*. is fulfilled and Jerusalem is 'trodden down by the nations' as predicted in Luke XXI: 24). The most likely itinerary for Jesus' movements on the night he was arrested and the morning when he was crucified thus seems to be as suggested in Ill. 104.

Execution

Jesus, together with the two robbers now led away with him, is to undergo the death by torture that some ancient writers regarded as the next most terrible after burning alive. Others, Cicero among them, said that it was unfit for free men, indeed that it was the most brutal and dreadful of the punishments which could be given to a slave. Because of its long-drawn-out agonies the executioners, as we have seen, always scourged the prisoners severely before crucifying them, in order to weaken their resistance and cause them to die sooner. Paradoxically, the scourging was introduced for reasons of mercy, and for the same reason was carried out with the most severe type of scourge, the *flagellum*.

The little we know about crucifixion in the ancient world has recently been amplified by the discovery at Giv'at ha-Mivtar, about a mile and a half north of the Old City of Jerusalem, of a tomb which contained in one of its stone ossuaries the bones of a man who was crucified when he was twenty-four to twenty-eight years old, at a time in the Second Temple period. Professor Haas of the Hebrew University's Department of Anatomy, after a concentrated study of the remains, discovered that in this case the upright stake of the cross was provided with a smallish seat-piece that was designed to prevent the prisoner collapsing, and thus dying sooner, as shown in Ill. 106.

105 (overleaf) The west wall of the Old City seen from the south-west. On our theory the Way of the Cross would lie between the Citadel in the foreground (arrow), where Jesus was condemned by Pilate, and the site of the two-domed Holy Sepulchre Church beyond (arrow), which was Golgotha

The feet were secured to the cross by a block of wood and a nail about 18 centimetres (7 inches) long which passed through the wooden block and the two heel-bones and was fixed in the stake of the cross, which was in this case made of olive wood. The upper part of the body was unsupported except for the nails which pierced the forearms (passing between the radius and ulna) and held them to the cross. The shin-bones of this skeleton were broken, apparently with some implement such as a mallet, like the legs of the thieves (John XIX : 32) crucified with Jesus. Possibly this victim was one of the two thousand Jews crucified by Varus during Jesus' childhood.

At what time of day was Jesus fixed to his cross? Mark XV : 25 tells us at the third hour, meaning the hour which began at about 7.35 a.m. In view of the time-table this would be possible, especially if Mark could mean towards the end of the hour. John, in whose time-table the Passover meal has still to be eaten, is probably writing with the object of presenting this Friday as the day when, in the afternoon, the Passover lambs would have to be killed. He tells us (XIX : 14) that at about the sixth hour Jesus' trial was ending in the Praetorium, which is to say the hour beginning at 10.45 a.m., and the Mishnah (*Pesachim* 5 : 1) says that the Passover offering was slaughtered at half after the seventh hour, meaning at about 12.15 p.m. At whichever time it was, three details have ancient parallels: the act of offering Jesus wine containing myrrh, which is mentioned in the Talmud (*B. Sanhedrin* 43a) as an act of mercy sometimes performed by the women of Jerusalem; the sharing of his clothes among the soldiers responsible for the execution, recognized in Roman Law (and mentioned in *Digest* 48 : xx : 6); and the display of a notice stating the nature of the crime (as in Suetonius, *Caligula*, 32).

On the cross Jesus is mocked, and there takes place what appears to be the final conflict. It is revealing to see the identity of the mockers. For Mark they are 'the passers by' (XV : 29), possibly recalling Lamentations I : 12 and II : 15 where the same Greek word is used in the phrase 'Is it nothing to you, all ye that pass by?' Mark goes on to identify as among them the 'chief priests and scribes' (XV : 31), to whom Matthew adds 'and the elders' (XXVII : 41). It is the same group here called 'the rulers' by Luke (XXIII : 35), who originally decided Jesus must die. The thieves crucified with him curse at him, and Luke adds some horseplay by the soldiers (XXIII : 36–38). At this point – the sixth hour, which began at 10.45 a.m. – the sun's light failed. An eclipse at Passover would be impossible, since the moon is full (or nearly so), but, as any one can testify who knows Jerusalem in

106 The position of crucifixion exemplified in a Jewish execution as it may have been in the time of Jesus' childhood

April, there can be heavy clouds and storms. This darkness continued till the ninth hour – beginning at about 1.50 p.m. – when, according to Mark (XV:37), Jesus uttered a great cry and expired. He adds that at this moment the curtain of the Temple was torn in half, a sign probably intended to mark the beginning of the destruction of the city and its Temple, thus beginning to fulfil Jesus' prediction in Luke XXI:24 and 25: 'There will be signs in the sun', and 'Jerusalem will be trodden down.'

Mark describes the centurion on duty saying of Jesus at his death, 'Truly this man was a son of God' (XV:39). Such a phrase probably implied only a mild degree of commitment when spoken by a pagan, but Mark doubtless included it in his Gospel because it was pregnant with meaning for the Christian reader.

The Tomb

Burial in the Holy Land was, and still is for members of its three major religions, a ceremony to be performed before sunset on the day of the death. But the religious Jews were particularly anxious that on this day the bodies of those who had been crucified should be buried before sunset, since it was the day before a Sabbath, which (at least according to John XIX:31) was also the first day of the feast of the Passover. The

Law specifically forbade that the body of an executed person should 'remain all night upon the tree' (Deuteronomy XXI: 22–23), and failure to observe this rule would be offensive indeed at the time of the festival. These Jews therefore requested of Pilate that the victims be given the coup de grâce (by breaking their legs) in time for burial before sunset. The coup de grâce was in any case intended as a merciful ending to the protracted torture of crucifixion.

It was already turning into evening (Mark XV: 42), so Joseph of Arimathea goes to Pilate (no doubt in the Palace) to obtain the necessary permission, and buys a winding sheet (Mark XV: 46) into which he and Nicodemus sprinkle spices. This Jewish custom was intended simply to make a pleasant smell and thereby render the death somewhat less alien and unpalatable, and was in no way comparable with the Egyptian practice of embalming, which preserved the body from decay. It was also the custom to rub the corpse with ointment and wash it, but the timing suggested by the Gospels hardly seems to allow for this. In fact the urgency was not quite so great for the washing as it was for the removal of the bodies from the cross, for there was a rule in AD 200, and perhaps already in Jesus' time, that even on the Sabbath 'They may make ready all that is needful for the dead body, and anoint it and wash it' (Mishnah, *Shabbath* 23:5). Indeed we see the women returning later on for this very purpose, though not on the Sabbath but on the following morning.

The rocky ground in the Jerusalem area makes grave-digging difficult, and the custom of burying so soon after death made it desirable to forestall any possible delays. Thus in Jesus' time all who could afford to dō so made themselves rock-tombs, for in case of death all that was needed was to remove the stone that covered the door, and to lay the body on a shelf. Since near Jerusalem we have hundreds of ancient rock-tombs from the general period of Jesus' lifetime we can form a good idea of the type of tomb that a prosperous man like Joseph of Arimathea would have made for himself.

The 'Tombs of the Kings' next to St George's Cathedral were made in about AD 50 for Queen Helena of Adiabene. She was converted to Judaism in Adiabene, which is the district round Arbela, 80 kilometres (50 miles) west of Nineveh. In AD 46 or 47 she came to live in Jerusalem, and made the great tombs in which eventually she was buried.

Since she was a convert we can be sure that her tomb conformed precisely with the Jewish religious regulations of the time, and this doubtless gives it strong affinities with that of Joseph of Arimathea who, as a member of the Sanhedrin (Mark XV: 43), helped make and enforce the regulations. Her tomb contains two types of recesses for receiving bodies. One is the *khokh*, a rectangular recess to be 'four cubits long, seven handbreadths high, and six wide' (Mishnah, *Baba Bathra* 6:8), which is equivalent to about 2 metres long, 65 centimetres high, and 55 centimetres wide (6½ feet by 25½ inches by 22 inches). This kind of tomb is shown in Ill. 107 to the left of the door, and its name *khokh*, which means 'oven', referred to its long narrow shape. Beside the *khokhim* there was a second type of recess, the simple shelf with an *arcosolium* ('arched ceiling') like the one shown in Ill. 109. A good many tombs have only recesses in the form of *khokhim*, but where there are both forms it seems likely that the *arcosolium* shelf would have been used at the time of the funeral. Later on, when the body was desiccated, it was removed to one of the *khokhim*, and at a subsequent stage, when all that was left was a skeleton, the bones were collected and placed in an ossuary, a stone box with a lid which would thenceforth be kept in some convenient part of the tomb. The removal of skeletons to the ossuaries meant that the shelves in the tomb would be clear and ready for the next funeral in the family.

The passage from the Mishnah just quoted also advises that a tomb chamber should have a floor area of 2 by 3 metres and a courtyard 3 by 3 metres 'to give enough space for the bier and its bearers'. Helena of Adiabene's was a royal tomb with a main chamber about twice as large as the chamber advocated in the Mishnah, but many other tombs are modest affairs. The outermost opening of the tomb complex would be the one to be sealed with a rolling stone, mainly in order to keep wild animals from entering. Some of these stones were light, such as the one shown in Ill. 108, and some considerably heavier, such as that at Queen Helena's tomb. Thus if the Christian tradition is correct we should envisage Jesus' tomb as falling within the general types we have examined, and if we have to choose between an *arcosolium* shelf and a *khokh*, we should probably opt for the former, since it would account for the sequence of events described in John XX:5–6. First the beloved disciple peers into the tomb from outside, seeing very much the same amount of the interior we can see in Ill. 109. Then Peter arrives, goes right inside, and can see everything on the shelf, including the part out of view at the near end where the headcloth may have been lying.

Luke XXIII:55–56 tells how women who were followers of Jesus watched the burial and then went home to prepare scents and myrrh. The stone that had been rolled against the tomb entry was therefore to be unrolled again.

107 (*opposite above*) *A chamber in the tomb complex of Queen Helena of Adiabene: on the left is a* khokh *and on the right a doorway leading into a smaller chamber with* arcosolium *shelves*

108 (*opposite below*) *The interior of a rock tomb at Bethphage, probably of the Byzantine period. The rolling stone can be seen in the entry*

109 (*left*) *An* arcosolium *in the tomb complex of Queen Helena of Adiabene*

110 (*below*) *The outer entry to the tomb complex of Queen Helena of Adiabene was sealed by a rolling stone. The stone in its slot is in the foreground and the entry is beyond*

Beyond Jerusalem

The Easter Experience

From the first generation onwards Christians understood Jesus' death as a release. This, for instance, is the kind of thought expressed by Peter in his first Letter when he says that Jesus was 'put to death in the flesh but was made alive in the spirit: in which he went and preached to the spirits in prison' (III: 19). Whatever, exactly, Peter may have meant by this, he is expressing the very belief which above all characterized Christianity in the first generation, namely that Jesus of Nazareth, who had truly died, had equally truly overmastered death.

The remaining passages in the four Gospels and much of the Acts of the Apostles declare this belief, and whether or not they are credible depends mainly on the trustworthiness of those who are making the declaration. For although the nature of the accounts is very unusual it may be that the authors are struggling to express something both wonderful and salutary. The writers are dealing with events that they regard, in some sense, as miraculous: thus the empty tomb is explained to the Maries by 'an angel of the Lord coming down from heaven' (Matthew XXVIII: 2). The resurrection itself and the Lord's appearances are deeply amazing, and so much beyond any normal everyday experience that we find normal reactions suspended. Thus the disciples remember Jesus telling Mary Magdalene not to cling to him (John XX: 17), and appearing in rooms where the doors were locked (XX: 19, 26), or disappearing (Luke XXIV: 31). Yet he is tangible, for he invites Thomas to touch him (John XX: 27). There seems to be some change in his appearance, for he is not always unmistakably recognized (Luke XXIV: 16, John XXI: 12). Here are memories overflowing with religious value and meaning, but hard to link with what we might term physical facts. For the present writer the main point of faith is 'that the Christ suffered this and entered into his glory' (see Luke XXIV: 26 and John XII: 16, XIII: 31, and XVII: 5). Any attempt to disentangle a sequence of tangible or 'objective' events from the resurrection narratives is bound to fail simply because it is inappropriate. Such events are out of reach for the reason, simple but profound, that they are indescribable. We are, however, easily within reach of the experience – vivid and heartening – of the group of men who, because they shared it, were moved to 'preach the gospel' (Romans XV: 19). To delve behind this experience (as opposed to appropriating it) is hardly likely to produce religious results.

We may nevertheless gain by analyzing some recurrent emphases in the Gospel accounts of this experience. The first is a circumstantial account of Mary Magdalene's arrival at the tomb with some other Galilean women: Mary, the mother of James, and Salome (Mark XVI: 1) or Joanna (Luke XXIV: 10). They find that the stone has been rolled back and are told 'He is risen, he is not here' (Mark XVI: 6). Mark says that they are also told that Jesus has gone before them into Galilee, and Matthew, who follows Mark here, adds after this passage his own original account of a farewell scene in Galilee. At that occasion Jesus tells the eleven disciples that they are to go 'to make disciples of all nations' and adds 'and, lo, I am with you always, even to the close of the age' (XXVIII: 19–20). Luke recounts some similar phrases about a message to be 'preached in Christ's name to all nations' (XXIV: 47), but says that they were spoken in Jerusalem. Indeed this location for the words is important to him, for he makes a point, both here and at the opening of Acts (I: 8), that this preaching is to have its 'beginning in Jerusalem'.

It was of fundamental importance to the early Church to have had the experience of seeing Jesus alive after death and burial. Thus in Luke's version of Jesus' farewell words to the disciples he speaks of his sufferings as Messiah and his rising from the dead, then adds 'You are witnesses of these things' (XXIV: 48). Earlier on – perhaps about twenty-five years after the crucifixion – Paul wrote that Jesus after the resurrection 'appeared to Cephas, then to the Twelve' (meaning the inner group of disciples), 'then he appeared to more than five hundred brethren at one time, most of whom are still alive, though some have fallen asleep. Then he appeared to James, then to all the apostles. Last of all, as to one untimely born, he appeared also to me' (I Corinthians XV: 5–8). Paul makes no distinction between his vision of Jesus on the road to Damascus and the visions experienced by the other witnesses which, we suppose, took place in the period immediately following the crucifixion. We cannot, however, be sure that this supposition is correct, for the Gospels tell us of two groups of resurrection experiences: those in Galilee, implied in Mark XIV: 28, XVI: 7 and mentioned by Matthew (XXVIII: 16), but described with a wealth of detail in the present ending of John's Gospel (XXI: 1–22), and those in Jerusalem. This latter group is described by Luke (who also speaks of the experience near Jerusalem on the road to Emmaus) and by John, in what seems to have been the original ending to his Gospel (XX: 19–29: note verses 30–31).

The name Emmaus was fairly common in Palestine, and it is by no means obvious which one the Gospel of Luke is describing. Let us start by asking how long it seems that it took to get to Emmaus. Two disciples set out from Jerusalem some time on the day of the resurrection. Luke does not say when, but we assume that it was well after dawn, since they already knew about the empty tomb and the vision of angels (Luke XXIV: 22–23). They are joined by a stranger, and when the outward journey is complete the disciples ask the stranger to stay with them 'for it is getting on for evening, and the day has passed its best'. They all go in for a meal: they recognize the Lord, and 'he disappeared from them' (Luke XXIV: 31). At that they go back to Jerusalem, and find the Eleven not yet gone to bed, but sitting together. The fourth-century Palestinian manuscripts of St Luke disagree with most of the others in reporting the distances from Jerusalem to Emmaus. Where other manuscripts (presumably including those used by the Palestinian scribes) state that the village was 'sixty stades' away they give 'a hundred and' before the word 'sixty'. Sixty stades, if we count the stade as 195 metres (600 feet) is 11.5 kilometres (7½ miles), and 160 stades is about 31 kilometres (19½ miles). Let us assume that the Palestinian scribes made the change because they knew of no Emmaus 60 stades from Jerusalem. But everyone was familiar with the city Emmaus on the way to Joppa, which was awarded the name of Nicopolis (Victory City) by the Roman Emperor Elagabalus early in the third century A D. This is now Khirbet Imwas. The timing that is implied by the Gospel, however, makes it very hard to accept that this can be correct, even though all who visited or wrote about Palestine from the fourth century to the seventh were familiar with this Emmaus. The story of the journey out, the meal, and the journey back (which finished before the other disciples had gone to bed) is not recounted as if there was any haste. Now 31 kilometres (19½ miles), which is the distance to Emmaus-Nicopolis, involving a change of altitude of 500 metres (1,600 feet), is

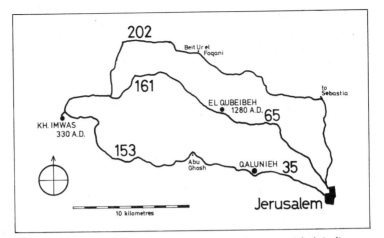

III Some suggested sites for the New Testament Emmaus with their distances from Jerusalem in stades (or furlongs). A stade here is 195 metres (600 feet)

the equivalent of a whole day's journey. To have gone twice as far, one way uphill, in a single day would have involved haste and energy that would surely have been remembered and reflected in Luke's narrative.

Emmaus-Nicopolis then, though it was the first place taken to be the New Testament Emmaus by local Christians, was mistakenly identified. In the seventh century AD this Emmaus virtually disappeared, owing to a serious outbreak of plague that began there in AD 639. Hence the Crusaders and their successors in the Latin kingdom of Jerusalem knew of no obvious place for Emmaus and seem simply to have measured a distance on the roads of sixty furlongs from Jerusalem and taken the nearest village to be Emmaus. One of these was el Qubeibeh, which is first mentioned as the New Testament Emmaus only in 1280, and the other was Abu Ghosh. There is no evidence that any one had regarded either of these sites as Emmaus before the arrival of the Crusaders.

It seems unlikely that the Emmaus of the New Testament should be sought at Nicopolis, now Khirbet Imwas, which is too distant. Equally Abu Ghosh and el Qubeibeh have nothing to recommend them except their distance from Jerusalem. We are therefore left with a fourth possible site, a place which the Mishnah tells us 'used to be below Jerusalem called Motza', which was a source of willow branches (*Sukkah* 4:5). Presumably the words 'used to be' imply that

Motza had for some reason ceased to exist by AD 200, when the Mishnah was written down.

The name Motza as it is written in Hebrew may very well be the same name as the name Amassa, which occurs in the Latin version of Josephus (*War* 7:217). But in the Greek version the name is *Ammaous*, which we may regard as identical with the *Emmaous* of the Greek New Testament. In this passage of *The Jewish War* Josephus tells of eight hundred veterans of the first Jewish-Roman War to whom Titus in AD 70 assigned this Ammaous, which, he tells us, was thirty stades from Jerusalem. Why was this site not known to the fourth-century Palestinian scribes of the New Testament? Probably because by his time the place had already been renamed 'Colonia', the name it retained until its destruction in 1948. Josephus is more or less correct in telling us that this site is thirty stades from Jerusalem.

For the site of Motza-Colonia we can argue the reasonable distance and the name. The disciples could certainly have completed two journeys of about 6.5 kilometres (4 miles) each in a day, and the thirty stades seem to take us to a place which had the right name in Jesus' time, even though it was later supplanted by 'Colonia'. But the distance does not agree with the biblical text, either for the generally accepted 'sixty' or the Palestinian 'one hundred and sixty' stades. Motza-Colonia is therefore not certainly the Emmaus of the New Testament, but if it were, then both distances in our biblical texts were wrong. To the present writer this seems the most probable solution to the problem. Certainly it would explain the failure of the early Christians to rediscover Motza-Colonia in their search for Emmaus.

When the two disciples had recognized Jesus in Emmaus they returned as fast as they could to the place in Jerusalem where the disciples were gathered. In later times Christians believed that this place was the house which had formed the disciples' headquarters in Jerusalem from the time of the Passover to Pentecost, or, to be more precise 'the upper room where they were staying' (Acts I:13). Possibly this was the 'house of Mary, the mother of John whose other name was Mark' (Acts XII:12).

In the fourth century AD Christians believed that all the oldest buildings in Jerusalem were on the western hill, which they had mistakenly come to call Mount Sion. Seven synagogues there are said to have survived into the time of Hadrian, together with 'a few houses, and the church of God, which was small.' Epiphanius, the Bishop of Salamis who wrote this, remembered that one of the synagogues could still be seen in the reign of Constantine, and he may well have seen it

112 The modern group of buildings on Mt Sion seen from the north

himself, since he lived in Palestine for about the last two decades of Constantine's reign. But the little church had most likely been destroyed by Diocletian, at a time when it was probably the only one in the city in AD 303. Later in the fourth century, when it had been rebuilt on a larger scale, it was called 'The Upper Church of the Apostles', and in the middle of the fifth it is mentioned in the Jerusalem Liturgy of St James as 'the holy and glorious Sion, the mother of all the Churches.' The Jerusalemites believed not only that the Apostles had used a building on that very site (which may explain why one of its principal treasures was the Chair of St James the Just), but that in that building the Church as we know it was first constituted by the visitation of the Holy Spirit at Pentecost.

The original building, probably destroyed by Diocletian, is likely to have been a house adapted for worship, but by AD 348 it was a church and, if this is the building shown in about AD 600 on the mosaic map at

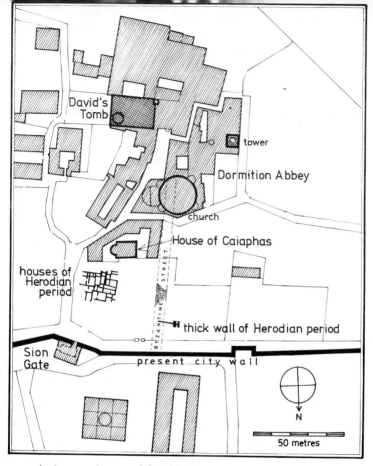

113 Ancient remains concealed within the modern group of buildings, Mt Sion

Madaba, it was of considerable size. The site of this church, on the summit of what Christians named Mount Sion, is just outside the city walls at their south-west corner. It is today occupied by a closely knit group of buildings surrounded by cemeteries, which can be seen in Ill. 112 and Ill. 113. They are viewed from the north with the city wall at the bottom and the Sion Gate projecting inside it on the left. The large tower, surrounded by scaffolding, and the conical roof belong to the Dormition Abbey (1906) and Church (1900), which were built beside the large complex of buildings known until 1948 as Nebi Da'ūd, 'The

Prophet David'. One of these buildings, according to a late Jewish and Muslim tradition, contained David's tomb, and the domed cupola directly above the tomb can be seen on the left end of the roof of the building beyond and to the left of the Dormition Church: there is a minaret at the right of this roof, and large battlements round it. Beneath this roof are the oldest structures in the area, apart from those revealed by excavations carried out in the past hundred years.

Between the Dormition Church and the present city wall Dr Magen Broshi has been making some important discoveries in recent years. One is a stretch of Byzantine paved street, and to its right (on the diagram, but not visible in the air photograph) is a short stretch of thick wall of the Herodian period, which may have belonged to a public building. On the left of the paved street is a concrete platform, recently arranged so that it would cover and protect the archaeological remains below. They comprise domestic buildings that were built and then redeveloped in the course of the reign of Herod the Great. Mount Sion was certainly a heavily populated area then and in Jesus'

114 The present buildings on Mt Sion seen from the north-east. David's Tomb is in the two-storey building in the foreground, beneath the dome directly to the right of the trees at the foot of the picture

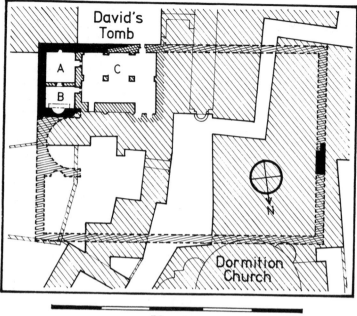

115 The probable area of the Church of Holy Sion. David's Tomb is at the north end of chamber B. The solid black indicates the remains of ancient walls, probably of the Byzantine period

lifetime. It is therefore possible that the Apostles' headquarters was there, and that it survived for a considerable period.

Let us therefore examine more closely the so-called 'Tomb of David' and the building that contains it, which is the two-storey building with the cupola in the near corner shown in Ill. 114. The cenotaph of David is on the ground floor (the long rectangle below the letter B on Ill. 115), and there is a second cenotaph on the floor above. Hence David's Tomb properly so called is the end of the building marked by the cupola on the roof and containing rooms A and B. To the west (or right) of these rooms is the low room C with its heavy vaults supporting the fine pillared chamber above. This upper room is the Cenacle or 'Room of the Supper' which, although it is the oldest place where the Supper has been devotionally remembered, must have been built in its present style in the fourteenth century by architects from the Latin kingdom in Cyprus. There had been an earlier Cenacle, either in the same place or at least close by, but even so it is interesting to see on our diagram how the north wall of antechamber C is not continuous with the north wall of room B, with its niche. Just as the Tomb of David and the Cenacle represent two distinct commemorations, so too they seem to be architecturally separate. In room C there is nothing like the ancient and damaged masonry of the wall behind David's Tomb, which can be seen in Ill. 117, and appears to be the oldest wall in the neighbourhood.

Is this part of the building that was known as David's Tomb in the days of Herod the Great? This tomb is mentioned by Josephus but not its position, and also by St Peter (see Acts II:29), but thereafter no document refers to it until late in the tenth century A D, when a tomb of David is mentioned in a *Life of Constantine*. Thus there is probably no continuous tradition linking the Tomb of David which has been there since the Middle Ages with that of the Herodian period.

116 The Cenacle, traditionally on the site of the upper room of Pentecost and later believed also to have been the site of the Last Supper. It reached its present structural form in the fourteenth century, and some Muslim additions have been made since then. The room is above antechamber C of David's Tomb

Could the niche in the wall give us any idea of the purpose of the wall? The niches sometimes found in the walls of ancient synagogues are all in the wall nearest Jerusalem. But it would be strange for a synagogue to have survived into the Byzantine period in Jerusalem, when no Jews were allowed to reside there, and Epiphanius' language seems to rule out the existence of any synagogue there after Constantine's reign. The niches in synagogues that we already know are, moreover, all in the centre of the wall nearest Jerusalem. But the wall in David's Tomb that incorporates the niche was not a broad wall like the others we know. Indeed it is only 6 metres (19 feet) wide and the niche is not central.

It seems more likely that the wall was a short projection forming the exterior of an inscribed apse, as suggested in the church plan superimposed on Ill. 115. It will be seen that the north wall of chamber B is not continued in the north wall of antechamber C, and such projections belonging to the apse, being made of solid masonry, often contain cupboards or niches on the outside. In this case the ancient masonry would belong (as was first suggested by Father Hugues Vincent) to the Church of Holy Sion, as it was rebuilt sometime in the fourth century. This likelihood is increased by the proposed size of the church, as shown in Ill. 115, which is nearly identical in width with that of Constantine's Martyrium on Golgotha, and by the texture of the stonework shown in Ill. 117. It would appear that the masonry has been cracked by fire, and we know that the Persians set fire to the Byzantine Church of Holy Sion.

No structure on the site of David's Tomb need go back as far as the time of Jesus. Certainly the biblical text and the nearby Herodian remains leave open the possibility that the disciples used a house there or somewhere near, and it seems probable that the Church of Holy Sion earned its title 'Mother of all the Churches' in virtue of the belief that it was built on the same site as that of the earlier 'church of God which was small'. Thus the site may be that of the upper room where the disciples were staying before Pentecost, and therefore the place where they experienced Jesus appearing after his crucifixion, and also the coming of the Holy Spirit. As such it would indeed be the oldest place of Christian worship in the world, and would merit its title.

Both Luke and John describe how the disciples were gathered in the place where they were staying when Jesus appeared, standing there among them (Luke XXIV:36, John XX:19). Luke treats this as a single occasion but John combines it with his account of Thomas' confession of faith, and he presents Jesus as appearing once to the ten

117 The niche in the old wall on the north of David's Tomb. It was probably part of the Byzantine Church of Holy Sion, that was burned by the Persians, for it shows signs of fire damage. The ornaments in front of the niche are standing on top of the cenotaph of David, about 2 metres (6 feet) above the ground

disciples in Thomas' absence, and then a second time when Thomas is present. Both Luke and John report these as supernatural experiences ('they thought they were looking at a spirit', Luke XXIV:37; see also John XX:19). At the same time they firmly establish the point that he was real, and really the Jesus they had known before the crucifixion. Jesus thus invites the disciples to touch him (Luke XXIV:39, John XX:27) and takes food in their presence (Luke XXIV:30, 42, but not explicitly in John XXI:13).

The particular point thus established is hard for a modern reader to accept, particularly at a time when honesty seems to require the application of scientific criteria to statements of every kind. Yet there are some statements to which such criteria are inappropriate. It would for instance be absurd to apply them to exclamations or to poetry, or to emotional expressions of joy or grief. An experience can be 'real' in the sense that it is authentic, sincere, and important to the subject, and yet still remain beyond the grasp of present-day science. Why then, we may ask, should the Bible need to lay so much emphasis on the physical reality of Jesus' risen body? Would it not be enough that he has won a cosmic victory over the power of death? To the modern reader the abstract statement may indeed express a reality more immediately acceptable and understandable than the account of a physical resurrection. But it is hard to see how an abstraction of this sort could have been acceptable to the earliest followers of Jesus who, despite the Westernized society in which they lived, were at heart Galilean villagers, and non-Westerners. We cannot imagine them treating human beings as mortal bodies inhabited by immortal souls in the manner of the pagan philosophers of the West, and for them death was the end of soul as well as body. Thus if a person were to be conceived as rising from the dead the rising also must be soul and body, and anything less would not be resurrection. The point is made that Jesus' body is the same body that the disciples knew before the crucifixion and burial.

Despite the importance of this point it was also apparent to the earliest Christians that the person, though retaining identity after death and resurrection, was in some way also transformed. St Paul wrestles with the implications of this conviction in greatest detail in I Corinthians XV:35–55, and arrives at the position 'this perishable nature must be put on the imperishable, and this mortal nature must put on immortality.' He is saying that the 'resurrection body' is not (like a ghost) something less than the 'body of flesh', but something more.

From Earth to Heaven

Experiences of the risen Christ as recounted in the New Testament seem all to belong within a limited period after the resurrection, excepting of course the experience of Paul on the road to Damascus. Luke describes this limited period as lasting forty days (Acts I:3), and thenceforward Jesus is conceived as being seated on high at the right hand of God (Romans VIII:34) until the time of his final appearing (I Peter I:7). This is the picture which emerges from almost all the books of the New Testament with the notable exceptions of the Gospels of Mark (assuming XVI:19 to be an addition) and Matthew.

How is it that the risen Jesus was at one time appearing to his followers on earth and then believed to be in Heaven? How should we picture the transition? Surely this question can only be asked in cosmic terms – how was he who was 'manifest in the flesh' then 'taken up in glory' (I Timothy III:16)?

When Jesus meets Mary Magdalene in the garden at dawn on the first day of the week he tells her, 'I am ascending to my Father . . . to my God' (John XX: 17). In the mind of John the resurrection (rising from the dead) and the Ascension (going to the Father) may be a single concept, or perhaps be seen as a single process taking place on that first day of the week. Luke may have been thinking in the same terms, for in Chapter XXIV he describes the resurrection and the final parting at Bethany as if both events took place on a single day. Here then is one way of picturing the transition from 'flesh' to 'glory'. But we learn from Luke that a 'parting scene' is not inconsistent with a further appearance of Jesus to Paul.

The obvious way of expressing the transition is to put it in terms of moving up from earth into the sky, and Luke adopts this expression when he says that Jesus 'led the disciples out as far as Bethany . . . parted from them and was carried up into heaven' (XXIV: 50–51), or speaks of 'the day when he was taken up' (Acts I: 2). Some scribes of ancient manuscripts of the New Testament were embarrassed by the apparent inconsistency between these passages and Luke's account of the Ascension in Acts I: 9–10, and for this reason (we imagine) simply omitted them. But there seems no reason to doubt that Luke wrote both versions, and their inconsistency (which is real) is very likely due to additional testimonies to the Ascension, reported to him between the time he wrote the Gospel and the Acts of the Apostles.

The narrative of Acts I: 9–10 not so much describes the heavenly exaltation of Jesus as his final parting from the Apostles, and this stress is further made by the message of the two men in white robes (verse 11) that Jesus 'will come in the same way as you saw him going into the sky.' The physical ascension of Jesus (which is implied and made necessary by a physical resurrection) is not itself his heavenly exaltation, but it is certainly a pointer towards it or, as we might put it, an 'acted parable'.

Where did the Apostles experience this final parting? Though Luke says at the end of his Gospel that it was at Bethany no later pilgrim or Jerusalem Christian ever seems to have remembered it there. Nor indeed was it in the place where the Jerusalemites first commemorated it, for this was none other than the Eleona Cave, and Acts I: 10 demands that the place of the Ascension should be in some open place from which it was possible to look up into the sky.

The unsuitability of the cave as a 'scene' for the Ascension no doubt led to plans to build a sanctuary for the Ascension elsewhere. And it may well be that it had been more convenient (or safe) to remember the

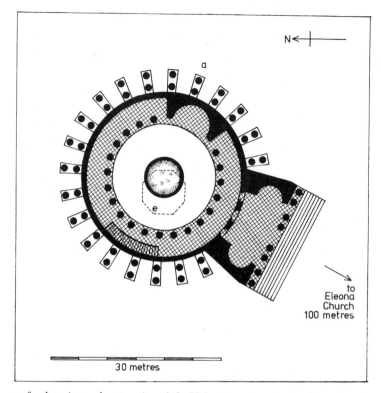

to
Eleona
Church
100 metres

30 metres

118 A conjectural restoration of the Holy Ascension, the circular colonnade erected to surround the rock of the Ascension. Its founder was Poemenia, a noblewoman who came on pilgrimage to Jerusalem in about AD 390

Ascension in the cave even though those who did so believed that Jesus had actually been taken up from the nearby hillock. At any rate this hillock (the Imbomon) seems to have been used for commemorative services even before any building was erected there. The building was added in about AD 390, and its site can be seen in Ill. 90, which, beyond the remains of the Eleona Church, shows an irregular roundish courtyard containing a medieval domed building. This courtyard is a degraded version of an octagonal cloister constructed during the period of the Latin kingdom, and this in turn was the successor of the original structure of the late fourth century.

Poemenia, the wealthy pilgrim who founded the sanctuary, arranged it specifically to enable those inside to see the sky. Ill. 118 presents a guess at its arrangements, which is derived on the one hand from early descriptions and a rough plan made in the seventh century, and on the other from the necessarily restricted excavations carried out by Father Virgilio Corbo. The area he could examine was all outside the wall of the courtyard, and contained the remains between the buttress marked (a) and the east wall of what may have been the porch. In other words our plan is based on very little evidence. At least we know that 'the Holy Ascension' was a colonnade surrounding a court which was open to the sky. In the middle the documents mention a patch of natural rock, the summit of the hillock, which was surrounded by a bronze grill. The position of the present domed structure is shown on our plan by the dotted line (e), and the present entrance to the courtyard is on the line of the ancient circular outer wall marked on our plan and immediately below it. All early visitors say that the original sanctuary, unlike the present domed building, had no roof over the central rock. The sanctuary was designed as a setting for meditation on earth and sky, and on Jesus' lordship in both.

Memories

When the disciples looked back on Jesus' ministry they seem mostly to have been asking what it meant to them as Jews. Jesus was Lord, Jesus was Saviour and Messiah. How was this to affect their attitudes and loyalties? While the majority of the members of the Christian group in Jerusalem were occupied with questions like these an energetic mission was going on elsewhere, and the Churches that soon came into being in Syria, Asia Minor, Greece, and Rome itself seem to have displayed a vigour not evident in the Jerusalem Christian community. In the meanwhile the siege of Jerusalem in AD 70 further weakened a Church which had not yet proved strong; and when Hadrian exiled Jews from the Jerusalem area in AD 135, most of the indigenous Christians, being of Jewish birth, must have become refugees. At that point Eusebius states that there began in Jerusalem a succession of bishops of Gentile stock, meeting, no doubt, in the little church building on Mount Sion.

If this bird's-eye view of the first century and a half of Christianity in Jerusalem makes depressing reading we may imagine how hard it was for the Church leaders of the time to explain to their visitors how it could be that in Jerusalem, of all places in the world, Christianity could be so small and weak. They must have had the additional difficulty of explaining how the Jerusalem Christians – a group which in the New Testament is so obviously composed of Jews – had come to be all or mainly Gentile.

For the Jerusalem Christians both these factors enhanced the apologetic value of the holy places, because they helped to explain how the Jerusalem Church, small as it was, was truly the spring from which the river of Christianity had burst out into the world. And already in the early second century (if we are to believe Eusebius) Christians were aware of the location of Jesus' tomb and (as we are told by Justin) went to visit the cave in Bethlehem where he was said to have been born.

Even without this apologetic motive for valuing the holy places the Jerusalem Christians could not have helped knowing some of them. Places such as Gethsemane, Bethesda or the Temple area were well known landmarks, sufficiently identified by their names alone; and the place of Jesus' crucifixion would have been common knowledge to several thousand people, for it had been a public execution and not a mystical experience, revealed only to initiates. Any visitor who wanted to know where the Cross had stood would, until about AD 100, have been able to find people in Jerusalem who could remember the day of the crucifixion, and would know the precise whereabouts of the tomb provided by Joseph of Arimathea. This direct memory was of special value if, as is probable, Herod Agrippa redeveloped the area in AD 44.

Besides the places where events mentioned in the New Testament had actually taken place there were evidently places set aside for prayer. Such was the cave on the Mount of Olives, which is first mentioned about a century before Constantine erected a church over it. It cannot have been the place on the Mount of Olives envisaged in Luke's account of the Ascension in Acts I:9–10. But it probably served as a small sanctuary in which Christians could meditate on all the New Testament events that took place on the Mount of Olives. Perhaps there were other such places being used before Christianity finally came out into the open under Constantine. If there were, we have no firm evidence about them

The Holy Land offered unique possibilities for Constantine, the first Roman emperor actively to favour Christianity. How did he make use of them within the framework of his imperial policy? Any answer to this question is certain to have been worked out by Constantine with his friend Eusebius, Bishop of Caesarea. The basis of the policy adopted was to display and adorn three sites, 'the three holy caves' shown in Ill. 119. In these three places was distilled the essence of Christian belief about Jesus, as demonstrated by the words written against them in the diagram, for these belong to one of the earliest baptismal services known, and were therefore intended to sum up the Christian's basic belief about Jesus. The policy was therefore to develop the three sites in such a way as to express straightforwardly the essentials of the Christian faith, a faith that the Emperor hoped would secure unity for his empire.

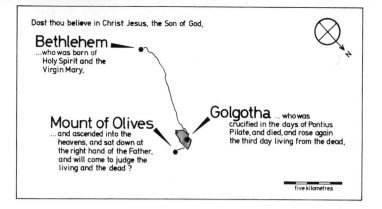

Dost thou believe in Christ Jesus, the Son of God,

Bethlehem
...who was born of
Holy Spirit and the
Virgin Mary,

Mount of Olives
... and ascended into the
heavens, and sat down at
the right hand of the Father,
and will come to judge the
living and the dead ?

Golgotha ... who was
crucified in the days of Pontius
Pilate, and died, and rose again
the third day living from the dead,

five kilometres

This overall policy as it applied to Jerusalem points to an interesting secondary motive on Constantine's part. Ill. 120 first shows Jerusalem in the days of Herod the Great, or as an exclusively Jewish city, as we have seen. Its religious focus was the Temple, and although we have examined some other sites from that period, which are of religious value to Jews, orthodox or less orthodox, no other religion seems to have had any public cult. After the first Roman-Jewish War the Temple was destroyed, and after the second Jews were banned from the city. Hadrian then devised a city plan with an entirely new religious emphasis, and his policy had both short- and long-term advantages. By the end of the second Roman-Jewish War Hadrian's relationship with the Palestinian Jews was bitter: he therefore left the Temple in ruins (as indicated on the second map of Ill. 120), and erected on the site a statue of himself. This negative treatment of the Temple site was balanced by the erection of a Capitol with the official Roman temple to Jupiter Capitolinus, Juno, and Minerva in another part of the city. Where the treatment of the old Temple site declared to the world the impotence and rout of Judaism, the Capitol proclaimed the victory of Rome and its gods.

It may well be true, as Eusebius says, that Hadrian chose the site for the Capitol because it was already of special significance to the Christian community (which had mostly been expelled with the Jews). If so then the short-term objective would be to obliterate Christianity. But it is hardly likely that Hadrian would have intended to do this when on another occasion he insisted that Christianity in itself was not a punishable offence. Nor had Hadrian forgotten the potential importance of the empire-wide Jewish diaspora, whose support he or his successors might at some time need. By leaving the Temple site in ruins he left open the possibility that at such a time the Jewish Temple

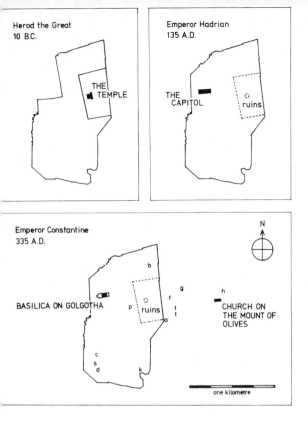

Herod the Great
10 B.C.

THE TEMPLE

Emperor Hadrian
135 A.D.

THE CAPITOL

ruins

Emperor Constantine
335 A.D.

N

BASILICA ON GOLGOTHA

b

g

h

p   ruins   f

t
t

a

CHURCH ON
THE MOUNT OF
OLIVES

c
s
d

k

one kilometre

119 (opposite) The 'three holy caves' that Constantine adorned in the Holy Land, and their meaning. The words are those of an early baptismal creed

120 The Holy Places in Jerusalem: Jewish, pagan, and Christian

might be rebuilt, and about two centuries later the Emperor Julian availed himself of this very opportunity. The Jews started rebuilding their Temple, even though eventually they were unable to complete it.

Constantine, had he so wished, could have done what the Crusaders were to do to the city eight hundred years later, and turned the Temple area into a sanctuary for Christians. But he chose otherwise, paradoxically re-establishing the pattern of Hadrian's policy, though at the same time substituting Christianity for paganism as the official religion of the empire. His city plan proclaimed the triumph of Christianity in contrast to the continuing impotence of Judaism.

Long before the development of this official policy Christians in Jerusalem had been developing an unofficial topography. Thus the Pilgrim of Bordeaux, who visited Jerusalem in AD 333, was shown all the places marked on the third map of Ill. 120. He went to see the pools

179

at Bethesda (b) and Siloam (k), the ruins of Pilate's Palace (p) and of David's (somewhere near d), and the pinnacle of the Temple (a). Up on Mount Sion he was shown the ruins of the House of Caiaphas (c) and an ancient synagogue (s), no doubt the one mentioned by Epiphanius of Salamis, but he does not mention any church there. Perhaps it had been destroyed but not yet rebuilt in AD 333. Down in the Valley of Jehoshaphat he saw the monuments (t, t) now called the tombs of Absalom and Zechariah, but according to him belonging to Isaiah and Hezekiah; he was shown the palm tree from which the branches were plucked at the triumphal entry (f) and the Gethsemane rock (g) at which Jesus had been arrested. On the Mount of Olives he reports that he saw the church Constantine had built over the cave and a hillock (h) at which, so far as we can tell, he believed that Jesus had been transfigured (see Mark IX : 2–13). The only other church he mentions is the one Constantine built on Golgotha.

If we compare this topography with that of modern Jerusalem it is simple indeed, and particularly in two ways. There is hardly a holy place in Jerusalem today which has not had a church or chapel built over it, yet for this pilgrim there were only two churches in the whole city. Then again all the places he mentions (apart from a bizarre and legendary assortment inside the Temple area) are related to incidents recorded in canonical books of the Bible, whereas a fair number of the holy places of today are related to apocryphal incidents.

The Church of The Holy Sepulchre

Of all the holy places in Jerusalem the site called Golgotha has always been regarded by Christians as the most important. Unfortunately its history is also the most complicated, and what follows is only an outline. The site may well be the very place where Jesus was crucified and buried, and where Mary Magdalene met him on the morning of the first day of the week. It is today occupied by the church with the two domes which appears in Ill. 121. The most easterly part of the church today is a crypt, which is more or less in line with the tall white tower with a pyramidal roof, attached to the modern Lutheran Church of the Redeemer. But in the time of Constantine the buildings began at the larger of the two domes on the right, and extended left as far as Khan ez Zeit Street, which runs up the photograph on the left-hand side. The site of Constantine's religious buildings may well have been identical with that of Hadrian's Capitol, and Jesus' tomb (or the Holy Sepulchre) has its site below the larger dome.

*121 The block containing the Church of the Holy Sepulchre seen from the north.
The site of the tomb itself is beneath the larger of the two domes, and the original
church buildings reached as far as the arrow indicates*

*122 (overleaf) The Church of the Holy Sepulchre from the north. The area
beyond the present Church was the forum of Jerusalem from the time of Hadrian up
to and perhaps after the time of the Latin kingdom. It is now occupied by the
Lutheran Church of the Redeemer on the left (arrow) and the shopping centre
called the Muristan on the right (arrow)*

123 A model of the site of the present Church and forum from the north before
being enclosed by the city wall. The hillside on the right, with tombs cut into it,
the central rock outcrop, and the cistern (arrow) existed before AD 44. The
position of the city wall behind them is conjectural

124 Hillside from the east, showing entries to rock-tombs (arrows)

125 Impression of Hadrian's Capitoline temple, covering the tombs in the
hillside, from the east. Like the temple, the smaller building is an imaginary
reconstruction, representing the 'basilica', or market control building, in the
forum

The history of the site is most simply illustrated by means of a highly simplified model, and the position of the various elements can be seen by comparing Ills. 122 and 123, of which the latter shows some elements present on the site at the time of Jesus' crucifixion and burial. The whole site slopes down from the west side (right) to the east, and we may imagine a small hill at the west. Into its rock face were cut several tombs, and this rock face passed under the centre of the larger dome in the photograph.

A little way to the east (left) of this hillside was an outcrop of rock about 4 metres square (13 feet), which is on the ground floor inside the present church at a point between the smaller of the two main domes and the white cupola to its left, as visible in the photograph. To the left of that again is a deep rock cistern, now cut in half: this is beneath the trees to the left of the picture, and is approached through the crypt mentioned above. Somewhere between 'Hezekiah's Pool', the empty space surrounded by high buildings in the top right-hand corner of the photograph, and the minaret just beyond the present church used to run the city wall, but its precise location is not yet known, and the wall on the model is a mere guess. From the position of the top of the Lutheran tower the tombs in the hillside may have looked like the view of the model shown in Ill. 124. These, if tradition is correct, were incorporated in the area of the city within about fifteen years of Jesus' crucifixion, which according to Jewish custom would mean that the bodies they contained were re-buried elsewhere, and they were used no more as tombs. In AD 135 the site of these tombs was covered by Hadrian's pagan temple of Jupiter Capitolinus (see Ill. 125, which is again pure guesswork). At this period it is possible that the outcrop of rock with its straight sides may have formed the core to the left plinth in front of the temple, supporting a statue of Venus. But this suggestion is based on Jerome's assertion that a statue of Jupiter stood over the tomb and one of Venus over the rock outcrop (which he treats as Golgotha), and he may have been mistaken.

In about AD 326 the Capitoline temple was demolished, and to their unbounded joy the workmen removing the soil beneath it discovered the very tomb they had been told would be there. The next task was to display the tomb in a worthy manner. What sort of model would they have taken for such a task? There were hundreds of impressive models far away in Petra beyond the Jordan, but there were also a good many near at hand, including for instance the so-called 'Tomb of Zechariah'. This is simply a block of living rock that, after being isolated by a passage from the rock around it, is ornamented with carved pilasters

126 Removing the Capitoline temple revealed the tombs beneath. According to tradition one was Jesus' (arrow)

127 The tomb believed to have been that of Jesus (arrow) was isolated from the surrounding rock by Constantine's architects, in the manner used to create the Tomb of Zechariah

128 The earliest representations and descriptions of the little chapel formed from the rock suggest that it looked something like this in the Byzantine period. The rock cave containing the original tomb chamber is beneath the further roof with the cross on top

129 The tomb complex of the Bene Hezir in the Kidron Valley. The monument on the right, the nephesh, *now known as the Tomb of Zechariah, is fashioned in living rock*

and mouldings. Jesus' tomb was probably isolated by some comparable procedure from the rock of the hillside. The surrounding area was thus entirely changed, but it had already been buried for two hundred years under the foundation soil of the temple, and nothing of the garden of Joseph of Arimathea could possibly have remained recognizable until the time of Constantine. None the less the workmen would not have touched the most important part of the site, the tomb chamber itself, and soon after its discovery it probably looked very much as it had on that Friday afternoon when Jesus' body had been laid in it. The second tomb behind the one identified as that of Jesus was ignored by the builders, who eventually cut it in half and built a wall through it. The main tomb was decorated (perhaps as in Ill. 128), roofed, and gradually surrounded by buildings, as shown in Ill. 130. The building on the left represents the Constantinian baptistery, and its form is purely imaginary. But since the work of restoration in the church over the past sixteen years a great many new facts have been learned about the other buildings, including the Martyrium church at the bottom left of the photograph. This name,

130 The provisional Constantinian arrangements round the tomb, from the east. On the left, Constantine's baptistery. The high wall around the tomb masked the building works behind it. The large building, bottom right, is the Martyrium Church

131 The provisional Constantinian arrangements round the tomb, from the north. The rock used to commemorate Golgotha (arrow) lies against the west wall of the Martyrium Church

132 Constantine's architects planned to enclose the tomb in a rotunda (arrow), but it was finished after the Church's dedication in AD *335*

used elsewhere with other meanings, was judged particularly suitable for this site, because the Greek version of Zephaniah III : 8 reads, 'Wait for me, saith the Lord, on the day of my resurrection at the Martyrium.' The top of the rock outcrop which the Bordeaux pilgrim did and Eusebius apparently did not take to be Golgotha is just visible above the roof of the side-aisle, and its position is visible from another direction in Ill. 131. On top of the outcrop a commemorative cross was set up. This view of the model corresponds with part of Ill. 122, where the tomb is in the centre of the present rotunda below the larger dome, and the apse of the Martyrium (projecting westwards) occupies roughly the same area as the present apse (projecting eastwards) seen on the left of the smaller dome.

The Constantinian buildings were dedicated in AD 335 before the provisional arrangements had given way to the plan in its final form, and the account of this stage by Eusebius has recently been confirmed by archaeological discoveries. The tomb was at this stage surrounded by a high wall so that pilgrims, of whom there were doubtless many, could pray at the tomb without being disturbed by the building works in progress on the other side of the wall. The final stage of the work, which may have been completed only after Constantine's death, involved the enclosure of the tomb in a rotunda known as the 'Resurrection' or 'Anastasis' (see Ill. 132) which when it was finished (see Ill. 133) completed the new range of buildings. The whole complex looked something like the model as seen in Ill. 134, and of these buildings the outer wall of the rotunda and the near wall of the court on its left are still standing.

There is no evidence of any far-reaching changes in the structure of the Constantinian buildings for six and a half centuries, despite the damage done by the Persian invaders in AD 614. The end of the Constantinian buildings came in 1009 as the result of a deliberate attempt to obliterate them (and through them Christianity) on the part of the mentally sick Caliph Hakim. Up to his time the interior of Jesus' tomb had remained intact, but now Hakim sent orders that it was to be destroyed. The rock of the tomb was hewn down, and the Martyrium Church demolished.

No reconstruction was possible while Hakim remained Caliph. But the Byzantine authorities came to an agreement with his successors, and by 1048 had succeeded in restoring the surviving buildings and making a masonry replica to take the place of the original rock-tomb. Ill. 135 shows the general appearance of their buildings, and includes around the religious buildings various others that had been erected in

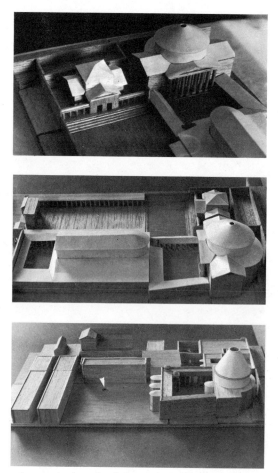

133 The finished rotunda completely enclosed the tomb. It was finished at the latest before AD *348*

134 Constantine's buildings as they stood from their completion, before AD *348, to the year 1009. The Persian ravages in* AD *614 probably caused little structural damage*

135 The reconstruction by the Emperor Monomachus, finished in 1048. The old cistern (arrow) was, in this period, believed to have been the place where the Wood of the Cross had been found

the neighbourhood, many of which encroached on municipal property, both in the streets (which thus became narrow) and in the forum. Some relics of the wide streets can still be seen, and show that the larger ones were 12 metres (40 feet) wide.

The credit for the restoration of the church buildings goes to the Byzantine Emperor Monomachus, who made no attempt to rebuild the Martyrium Church. This decision probably indicates the small size of the Christian community at that period. He restored the rotunda round the tomb, or rather round the replica, which had been placed there after Hakim had destroyed the original, and added an apse to the east of the rotunda so that it could be used as a church. He built or rebuilt the chapels on either side of the rotunda, one on the north and three on the south, and he raised the height of the courtyard wall and colonnades to the east of the rotunda. Golgotha now stood under its own roof, which projected into the courtyard at its south-east corner. To Monomachus we must ascribe also the new dome of the rotunda with its conical exterior. This formed one of the most characteristic features of the Jerusalem skyline until 1808, when it was finally destroyed by fire. Next to the Golgotha rock and its special roof, at the point where the east and south colonnades meet, a small cupola was built, which is still visible – the white cupola to the left of the two main domes in Ill. 122.

In 1099 the Crusaders poured into Jerusalem, and, though the Greek Patriarch and his bishops then left, the Greek monks and clergy remained in the church and continued to hold services. The Crusaders, or Latins, therefore added to the numbers attending services, and needed space for Latin services of their own, for the building restored by Monomachus was too cramped. The larger numbers made the provision of extra space a matter of urgent concern, but the Latins, who had come on their Crusades partly to save this very church, regarded the buildings and tomb with profound respect, and wished to alter as little as possible. Their solution was both ingenious and simple: they removed the new apse that Monomachus had added to the east wall of the rotunda (which they called the Church of the Holy Sepulchre) thus turning it into a large opening, and built a fine roof over what had been the open court.

The main approach to these buildings was by the Parvis, a court on the south side where the Latin kingdom architects constructed the splendid Crusader façade. It is still complete, except for the lintels of the main doors. These were removed in the 1930s and may now be seen displayed in the Rockefeller Museum.

136 *The Golgotha rock stands under the small roof (arrow), which projects into the courtyard from the far corner. In this reconstruction by Monomachus the court remained open to the sky*

137 *The main alteration the Crusaders made to the Church, restored not long before by Monomachus, was to construct a roof over the open court*

138 *The Church as restored in the Latin kingdom, viewed from the south*

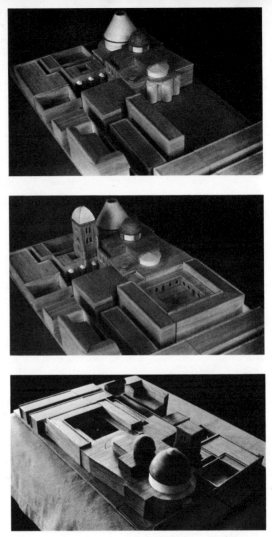

139 The Latin kingdom restorations seen from the south-east. At this stage, before the addition of the Canon's Convent, the outside of the three ambulatory chapels was still visible

140 The conventual buildings were added on the east of the Church to house the Augustinian Canons who were responsible for its services. The final Crusader addition to the church buildings was the bell tower

141 Present buildings at the Church of the Holy Sepulchre from the north-west

Accommodation was needed in the period of the Latin kingdom not only for congregations at prayer, but also for their clergy. The Augustinian Canons who served the church were therefore provided with a convent to its east, which masked the three chapels attached to the east end and blocked their windows, as can be seen by comparing Ills. 139 and 140. In the centre of the cloister of the new convent is a small dome. This lets light into the crypt below, which gave access to the ancient cistern, and in the Latin kingdom this was of special importance since it was then believed to have been the place where the Wood of the Cross had been discovered by Constantine's mother Queen Helena.

From the structural point of view very little has changed at the Church since the time of the Latin kingdom, as will be seen by a comparison of Ills. 141 and 143 with those examined above. All the major changes seem to have come about as the result of the great fire which gutted the Church in October 1808. The cone-shaped roof, which was wooden, fell in on top of the tomb, and the fire heated the masonry of the building to such a temperature that many stones were calcined, and became powdery, making the condition of the whole structure highly dangerous. Had it not been for the presence of mind of Comnenos of Mitylene, the Greek architect at the time, the Church might have collapsed, but he succeeded in stabilizing the pillars and walls by encasing them in plaster. The wooden dome was now replaced by one with a metal frame so that if there should ever be another fire the structure could not fall in.

Since 1959 the Greek, Latin, and Armenian Church authorities have been cooperating to restore the Church. They have now made the structure safe, largely by examining each stone and replacing any which have been calcined by an exact copy in sound stone. Thus in a short time we may expect to see the Church looking very much as it did on the day of its rededication by the Latins in 1149, apart from the metal-framed dome and the fact that the bell tower has lost a storey and a half from the top.

Holy Places

Modern Christians are accustomed to visiting historic houses, battlefields, and memorials. But most are not used to the idea of Christian holy places, and fear that there may be suggestions of idolatry in such phrases as 'Holy City' and 'Holy Land'. These, however, are biblical expressions, and are part of the view of life that

142 *The church buildings seen today from the south*

143 *The present buildings at the Church of the Holy Sepulchre seen from the north-west*

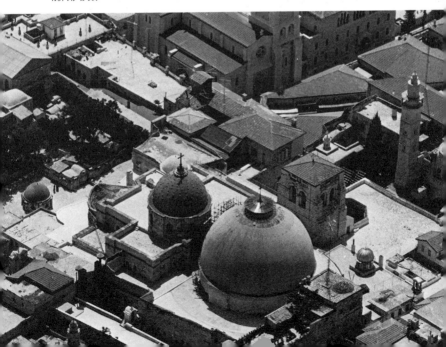

enabled men and women to think of God telling Moses, 'The place on which you are standing is holy ground' (Exodus III: 5), or made an early Christian writer call the place of Jesus' transfiguration 'The Holy Mount' (II Peter I: 18).

The principal aim of this book has not been to seek out or describe holy places. Rather it has been to describe the Jerusalem of Jesus' time as precisely as possible, especially in its physical aspects, such as climate, topography, and archaeology. If such factors had their effect on Jesus' message and ministry, then the more we know about them, the more likely we are to see Jesus' significance in his day. Even the apparently unimportant details may eventually contribute something valuable, and nothing is too prosaic to be ignored.

This aim is radically different from that of some of the Biblical archaeologists of the past, who hoped that the data gained would somehow 'prove the Bible true'. Thus Werner Keller's successful book has the illuminating title, *The Bible as History: Archaeology confirms the Book of Books*. Archaeology does sometimes confirm the Book of Books. Even so, there are a number of archaeological results that in no way confirm the Biblical accounts, but challenge them.

Both the archaeologists and the present author are seeking data. The aim is to assemble evidence that will add to the intellectual grasp of the past, and particularly of Jesus' time, and for such an enterprise we need all the discipline and precision we can achieve. Thus it is useful to know, if possible, the exact spot where a past event took place, since the location may add to our intellectual understanding of the event, and such exact spots can often be identified in Jerusalem. One is the Pool of Bethesda. Even a good approximation (like 'the Garden of Gethsemane') is far less satisfactory from this intellectual standpoint, despite the reasonable belief that the place where Christ was arrested is very probably near the Church of the Agony.

From this intellectual approach to sites, we may distinguish a devotional approach. It is not going to make a great deal of difference whether a site is scientifically acceptable if the visitor's only object is to pray at it. Indeed it sometimes proves easier to pray in an attractive place, like the beautifully kept Garden Tomb, than in the far less attractive Holy Sepulchre, regardless of the fact that one is likely to have been the place where Jesus rose from the dead and the other is not. Indeed one can pray anywhere.

Easy as it seems for twentieth-century Christians to distinguish the intellectual from the devotional approach to holy places, such a division is essentially modern, and born of our preoccupation with science. But, as we have already seen, the validity of the scientific method has its limits, and fails to touch many of the most vivid parts of our experience, such as poetry reading, love making, consoling, or promise keeping.

In ancient times, before the advent of scientific and experimental methods as we now know them, our distinction between the intellectual and the devotional was inconceivable. We cannot and would not abrogate our scientific ways of gaining knowledge. But there may still be advantages in understanding the pre-scientific approach to holy places. It is well exemplified in Eusebius' words when he describes the discovery of Jesus' tomb:

As layer after layer of the subsoil (beneath Hadrian's temple) was revealed, the venerable and most holy memorial of the Saviour's resurrection, beyond all our hopes, came into view. The Holy of Holies, the Cave, was like our Saviour 'restored to life' . . . by its very existence bearing clearer testimony to the resurrection than any words.

(Life of Constantine 3 : 28)

The language leaves the reader in no doubt that Eusebius regarded the tomb as holy, and he also says that it bore testimony. But he is not combining the devotional statements with anything intellectual in the scientific sense. The holiness and the testimony are not in tension with each other, partly because the testimony of the tomb is scientifically inadequate. In fact the finding of the tomb (even if it is truly the tomb of Jesus) no more proves that he rose from the dead than do the accounts in the New Testament. Rather the tomb and the Gospels – like the first Apostles – bear witness to the Gospel by proclaiming it. The tomb joins the other witnesses to the resurrection, and adds its affirmation to theirs.

If holy places are expected to proclaim rather than prove, they may serve a valuable purpose over and above the contribution they make within the strictly intellectual frame of reference. Most of them have some declaration to make. And amidst the diversity of authentic, approximate, and mistaken identifications there remains a nucleus of holy places which will stand the test of any investigation, whatever its scientific rigour.

Appendix

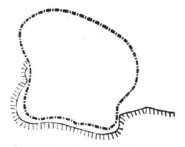

General Gordon's drawing of the contour of Skull Hill

General Gordon on Golgotha

I last wrote to you giving the four rivers of Eden, one of which was the Gihon on which Jerusalem was. I do not know if I then mentioned it was the Tyropœon Valley, which conclusion I came to ere I came to Palestine.

Golgotha. The morning after my arrival at Jerusalem I went to the Skull Hill, and felt convinced that it must be north of the Altar. Leviticus I: 11, says that the victims are to be slain on the side of the Altar northwards (literally to be slain slantwise or askew on the north of the Altar); if a particular direction was given by God about where the types were to be slain, it is a sure deduction that the prototype would be slain in some position as to the Altar: this the Skull Hill fulfils. With reference to the word 'askew' or 'aslant', we have the verse 'all the day long have I stretched out my arms to a rebellious people' (Isaiah LXV: 2). Draw a line from the centre of the Sakhra to the centre of the Skull; draw a perpendicular line to this line, at centre of skull; a cross on that line will embrace all the city and Mount of Olives, and be askew to the Altar.

The Latin Holy Sepulchre is west of the Altar, and therefore, unless the types are wrong, it should never have been taken as the site.

I pass by the fact of the tradition of Beth hat Selzileh, of the precipice of the tradition of its being the place Jeremiah wrote the Lamentations (which describes the scenes enacted there nearly 600 years afterwards, 'Is it nothing to thee, all ye that pass by' (Lamentations I: 12), &c., or the particularly suitable entourage of the place, for these things may be fanciful. I also will not hold to the fact that in the twelfth century St Stephen's Church was at the Damascus Gate, outside, and St Stephen was stoned nine months after our Lord's Crucifixion, and that it is unlikely that the Jews would have had two places of execution in nine months.

And I will come to the more fanciful view, that the mention of the place of Skull in each four gospels is a call to attention. Wherever a mention of any particular is made frequently, we may rely there is something in it; if the skull is mentioned four times, one naturally looks for the body, and if you take

Warren's or others' contours with the earth or rubbish removed showing the natural state of the land, you cannot help seeing that there is a body, that Schick's conduit is the œsophagus, that the quarries are the chest, and if you are venturesome you will carry out the analogy further. You will find also the verse (Psalms XLVIII), 'Zion, on the sides of the north;' the word 'pleura', same as they pierced His pleura, and there came blood and water, God took a *pleuron* from the side of Adam, and made woman. Now the Church of Christ is made up of, or came from, His *pleura*, the stones of the Temple came from the quarries, from chest of figure, and so on; so that fixed the figure of body to the skull.

Then by Josephus's account, as I read it, the Tower Psephinus was on the rocky point opposite the skull. Titus had his headquarters at the slaughter-house, 2 furlongs from the wall, viz., 300 to 400 yards, near the *corner* (note that corner, for it is alluded to in the 400 cubits broken down by Jehoash, king of Israel), and my placing of the walls and reading of Josephus would make his point of attack just where Schick's conduit enters the city east of Damascus Gate, or at the cisterns to east, where I think Agrippa's wall began. Mystically, the Roman Eagle should have gone at the Lamb of Zion by the throat, viz., Schick's conduit. However, I will not continue this, for if you please you can get the papers and plans from my brother. I would do them for you if you wish; I did them for Chaplin long ago. The camp of the Assyrians is the place where Nebuchadnezzar camped a month *after the fall of the city*, when he came to *burn the Temple;* it is this day which the Jews keep as the fast, not the day of *taking the city*.

Naturally, after discerning *the figure*, the question arose of Mount Zion, and of the boundaries; by studying the latter with the Septuagint there seemed no reason *by Scripture* to consider Ain Haud the *Enshemesh*. Septuagint has Beth Samos, and near Jebel el Tell is Kh. el Sama. Again, Gihon (being the Tyropœon) is to gush forth, and as the skull is the Altar, it is thence the two rivers, one to the Dead Sea, the other to the Mediterranean, are to come. At last Moses's blessing to Benjamin came in, 'he shall rest between His arms,' not his shoulders; so thus I brought the boundary up Gihon to Kh. el Sama.

Other reasons came to back this view,—

Nehemiah mentions town of Furnaces.

He also mentions throne of *Governor*.

Josephus mentions women's towers.

The word 'furnace' is derived from *fornex*, thence the connection. The tent Cozbi and Zimri went into was a *furnace*. Josiah broke down the high places built by Manasseh near the Gate of Governor, which were, no doubt, these same furnaces. Herodias lived at Jaffa Gate, and even to this day there are furnaces there I should think, for the troops are there.

This led to looking up the history of the Levites, &c., in Judges, of Gibeon, of mouldy bread, Nob, Gibeah of Saul, &c., and the result is as I have just noted, according to my ideas; but it is a matter of perfect indifference to us all, for these sites are in each of us.

During these studies, the potters' field comes up, and also the pool where Abner and Joab met, the field of the treacherous ones, and my idea is that round about the Serpent's Pool is the Tophet, Aceldama, Potters' field; that down the Valley of Hinnom is the Perez of David.

I will not bore you much longer than to say that, by my ideas,

Kuryet el Eneb is
- Kirjath-jearim
- Ramathaim-Zophim
- Armathaim
- Ramah, one of them
- Place of Saul's anointing
- Arimathæa
- Emmaus

and that Samuel was sacrificing to the Ark when Saul came to him.

Schick has been writing on these subjects for years, and he plaintively says, 'but how *am I* possibly to advance other views now?' In reality, in writing on these sites, no man ought to draw any cheques on his imagination; he ought to keep to the simple fact, and not prophesy or fill up gaps. If one wrote under cognomen α, and altered under cognomen β it would be all right; as it is now, a man under his own name cannot go right about face all at once. The Ark was built at Abu Shusheh by Noah, and floated up to Baris; only in A D 776 was it placed on Ararat, which is '*holy land*'. God said, 'Go to a mountain I will shew thee,' a mountain already consecrated by the resting place of the Ark. Noah offered on the rock his sacrifice. Look at Genesis and you will see (Genesis XI: 1), after the Flood they journeyed *eastward* to Shinar; you might go eastward from either Ararat or El Judi near Jesereb ebn Omar for ever before you reached Shinar. I will not bore you any longer, except to say that I think there are not many places far apart of interest in the Scripture way, and that these few are—

1. Nazareth and region of Tiberias.
2. Plain of Esdraelon.
3. Shechem.
4. Bethel.
5. Jerusalem.
6. Bethlehem.
7. Hebron.
8. Kuryet el Eneb, Philistia.
9. Jericho, Gilgal, Ammon and Moab, Dead Sea, Valley of Arabah.

C.G.

For Further Reading

General archaeological bibliography is usefully arranged in J. FINEGAN, *The Archaeology of the New Testament*, Princeton, 1969.

For geographical information see D. H. K. AMIRAN et al., *The Atlas of Israel*, Jerusalem and Amsterdam, 1970.

On the estimates of population for Jerusalem, see J. WILKINSON, 'Ancient Jerusalem: its Water Supply and Population', and A. BYATT, 'Josephus and Population numbers in First Century Palestine' in *Palestine Exploration Quarterly*, 1974, pp. 33–51, and 1973, pp. 51–60; and H. W. HOEHNER, *Herod Antipas, Society for New Testament Studies Monograph*, 17, Cambridge, 1972, pp. 52–53 and 291–95. Much of the material in my introduction is usefully discussed by Hoehner with very full references.

The best short description of what has been found at Capernum is S. LOFFREDA, *A Visit to Capernaum*, 3rd edition, Jerusalem, 1975.

A. ALON has produced an excellent illustrated non-technical work, *The Natural History of the Land of the Bible*, Jerusalem, 1969, but for deeper study the new *Flora Palaestinensis*, Jerusalem, 1975, is indispensable.

On the local style of Jerusalem architecture from 130 BC–AD 70 see *Jerusalem Revealed* (Israel Exploration Society), Jerusalem, 1975, pp. 14–20.

Y. MESHORER gives a useful introduction to the coins in *Jewish Coins of the Second Temple Period*, Tel Aviv, 1967.

N. Avigad's discovery of the street in the Jewish Quarter was reported in *Israel Exploration Journal* 20, 1970, pp. 129–40; and 22, 1972, p. 198. I have discussed the development of the street system in *Levant*, 1975, pp. 118–36.

On Herod's Palace and the three towers see C. N. JOHNS, *Quarterly of the Department of Antiquities in Palestine*, 14, 1950, pp. 121–90; and *Jerusalem Revealed*, pp. 54–64.

On the extent of the Antonia, see now P. BENOIT, 'L'Antonia' in *Harvard Theological Review* 64, 1971, especially pp. 158–61.

For details on the Jewish community in Jerusalem, see J. JEREMIAS, *Jerusalem in the Time of Jesus*, London, 1962.

On the Qumran community see J. MURPHY O'CONNOR, 'The Essenes and their History' in *Revue Biblique*, 81, 1974, pp. 215–44.

Of the many works dealing with the Temple some of the best and most up-to-date studies are those by MICHAEL AVI-YONAH and SAMUEL SAFRAI in *Encyclopaedia Judaica* 15, pp. 959–69.

Evidence available before the current campaign of excavations was reviewed by J. SIMONS in *Jerusalem in the Old Testament*, Leiden, 1952, pp. 381–436; and a summary of finds made by PROFESSOR MAZAR appeared in *Jerusalem Revealed*, pp. 25–40.

On the Temple establishment and Sanhedrin see J. JEREMIAS, *Jerusalem in the Time of Jesus*, especially part III, pp. 147–267.

The manner of making Sin – and Whole-offerings of birds is described in *Mishnah, Zebahim* 6: 4–5.

On Bethesda, see specially for a discussion of the textual problem, J. JEREMIAS, *Die Wiederentdeckung von Bethesda*, Göttingen, 1949, and for a recent summary of the archaeological evidence A. DUPREZ, *Jésus et les Dieux Guérisseurs*, Paris, 1970.

On Siloam, see H. GUTHE, *Zeitschrift des Deutschen Palästina-Vereins* 5, 1881, pp. 136–41, and F. J. BLISS and A. C. DICKIE, *Excavations in Jerusalem*, London, 1898, pp. 151–58 and pl. XVI.

On Bethany see S. J. SALLER, *Excavations at Bethany, (1949–53)*, Pubblicazioni dello Studii Biblici Franciscani (PSBF) 12, Jerusalem, 1957.

On the excavations at the Eleona Church on the Mount of Olives in 1910, see L. H. VINCENT and F. M. ABEL, *Jérusalem Nouvelle*, Paris, 1914, pp. 337–60 and pls. 34–9.

On the esoteric teachings of the scribes see JEREMIAS, *Jerusalem in the Time of Jesus*, pp. 237–43, and *The Eucharistic Words of Jesus*, 3rd edition, London, 1966, p. 125.

On the timing of the events of the Passion, see P. BENOIT, *Jesus and the Gospel*, vol. I of the English translation by BENET WEATHERHEAD, New York and London, 1973, especially pp. 95–98, 123–66.

On the ancient buildings on Mount Sion, see L. H. VINCENT and F. M. ABEL in *Jérusalem Nouvelle*, pp. 421–40, and J. PINKERFELD, 'David's Tomb' in *Bulletin of Louis M. Rabinowitz Fund* 3, Jerusalem, 1960, pp. 41–43 and pl. 9. For the recent excavations by DR MAGEN BROSHI see *Jerusalem Revealed*, pp. 57–60.

On the Church of the Agony at Gethsemane see L. H. VINCENT in *Jérusalem Nouvelle*, pp. 1007–13 and pl. LXXXVIII, and on the Gethsemane cave V. CORBO, *Richerche Archeologici al Monte degli Ulivi*, PSBF 16, Jerusalem, 1965, especially p. 85 and fold-out plans I and II.

The most enthusiastic defence of the authenticity of the House of Caiaphas at St Peter in Gallicantu is that of E. POWER, in L. Pirot (ed.), *Dictionnaire de la Bible (Supplément)*, vol. 2, Paris, 1934, cols. 737–745. Power is energetically refuted by L. H. VINCENT: see for example *Revue Biblique*, 1930, pp. 250–56.

On the location of Pilate's palace and the arrangements for his hearing of Jesus see P. BENOIT, *Jesus and the Gospel*, I, pp. 167–88, and his 'L'Antonia d'Hérode le Grand et le Forum oriental d'Aelia Capitolina' in *Harvard Theological Review* 64, 1971, pp. 135–67.

On the development of the Way of the Cross, see H. THURSTON, S.J., *The Stations of the Cross*, London, 1906.

For the skeletal remains at Giv'at ha-Mivtar see N. HAAS's article in *Israel Exploration Journal* 20, 1970, pp. 49–59.

On the Ascension see P. BENOIT, *Jesus and the Gospel*, I, pp. 209–253; and for the fourth-century colonnade see V. CORBO, *Richerche al Monte degli Ulivi, PSBF* 16, Jerusalem, 1965.

CH. COÜASNON's *The Church of the Holy Sepulchre in Jerusalem*, London, 1974, is an indispensable introduction to the new discoveries in the Church, and supersedes almost everything written previously.

Index